*Self-*Editing Essentials *for Fiction*

Polishing plot, characters, scene, and prose

Katie Chambers

Beacon Point LLC

ISBN: 979-8-9943102-3-6

Edited by Sara Judith Gustafson
Proofread by Robin Samuels of Shadowcat Editing
Cover design by Karolina Wudniak of Paperwing Studio
Interior design by Liz Schreiter

Library of Congress Catalog Number: 2026905070
First printing: 2026
www.beaconpointservices.org

To my husband, Gary Chambers:

It might be cliché to dedicate a book to a spouse, but hear me out. In my culture, people marry young, so by twenty-five I was already considered an "old maid." Gary swept me up right as I turned thirty, saving me from that perilous stage.

What he got in return was a woman who lives and breathes her work. Not working would feel like cutting off my right arm. Through building my company, raising three kids, and writing this book while scaling my business, he has stood by me—even when that meant evenings alone while I disappeared into my office after we had put the kids to bed.

None of this would be possible without his support and unwavering belief in my abilities. So, yes, I'm dedicating this book to him.

Acknowledgements

Writing a book is no joke, and doing it alone would be impossible. Many people contributed to this book, more than I can list here.

ALL MY EDITING CLIENTS

Thank you for trusting me with your manuscripts. I've grown as an editor through your books. Your stories gave me the skills and perspective that built the foundation for this book.

LAUNCH TEAM MEMBERS

Too many to name here, but they were my champions and supporters throughout my entire journey.

BETA READERS

When my beta readers first encountered this project as a simple PDF, they saw its potential and pushed me to expand it into the book you're holding now.

Souleiman Lazrak, a current client editing his debut novel.

Sarah Wayte, a copywriter and aspiring novelist writing her debut novel.

Ava Herman, a Seattle-based novelist writing an upmarket thriller.

Sarah Bailey, a fiction editor who majored in writing studies and minored in creative writing and writes middle-grade fiction and poetry.

Fallon Clark, fiction editor and author of a writing craft book on point of view.

Ross B Lampert, a three-time published science fiction author who started writing at age three and majored in English with honors in creative writing.

EDITOR AND PROOFREADER

Even editors need editors. Thanks to Sara Judith Gustafson for her excellent line editing, helping me when I was in a time crunch.

Thanks to Robin Samuels for her meticulous proofreading, saving me from a few embarrassing typos.

COVER AND INTERIOR BOOK DESIGNER

As someone with full aphantasia, I struggle with visual concepts, so I gave Karolina Wudniak of Paperwing Studio and Liz Schreiter very little to go on. I was basically like, "I don't know. Just make it look good." Well, the results speak for themselves.

Contents

TECHNICAL PASS   248

FEEDBACK PASS   292

CONCLUSION   296

GIFT FOR YOU   298

The Professional Editing Roadmap—A 6-Step Educational Email Course

INTRODUCTION

So . . . you wrote a book. An actual book. That's freaking amazing!

Guess what? I wrote a book too.

You might be thinking, *"Well, yes, Katie, I'm literally holding it."* Fair. But I needed to say it out loud because I never imagined this would be me. I've helped nearly 300 books come to life (as of 2025!), but until now, I hadn't written one of my own.

Doing so challenged and intimidated me, and yet I did it anyway. And so did you!

Before we talk about fixing anything, pause and acknowledge that. Take a breath. Do a tiny celebration—strike a superhero pose, pump your fist, whisper "I'm awesome," eat a slice of pie, or dance in your kitchen. However you do it, mark the moment: You finished a book.

Okay, but now real talk. I have a hard truth that you may already know: Writing the book is only the beginning. Now you're stepping into the part that often feels overwhelming—editing and revising. Even though good writing is rewriting, this stage terrifies most writers. It excites me because I live here. But you're not me. I'm not going to sugarcoat it: Self-editing is hard work and takes time.

Still . . . remember what you've already done: You wrote an entire book, something big and difficult.

You can do this part too. The benefits are well worth the effort.

And I'll guide you through the process. As a former English teacher, teaching is at my core and influences how I edit. In every book I work on, I model specific types of edits in the text and explain why I made the changes I did so my authors feel empowered in their choices. This editing style prepared me well to write this book.

> If you need additional help, appendices A and B contain even more resources, and my inbox is always open: kmchambers@beaconpointservices.org.

Why learn to self-edit well

"Writing without revising is the literary equivalent of waltzing gaily out of the house in your underwear."

— PATRICIA FULLER —

So, revise and edit your manuscript yourself because no one wants to see your underwear.

You might be thinking, *Wait a second, I'll have clothes over my underwear. My draft will be revised and edited by an editor. Editors edit; writers write. I'll catch a few typos and grammar errors and then pay an editor to take care of the rest.*

Editors absolutely can take care of a lot, but you can't grow as a writer without editing your own work. According to a quote often attributed to Ernest Hemingway, "The only kind of writing is rewriting."

You need to put some basic clothes on over your underwear before an editor can work their fairy godperson magic and help turn those clothes into a dashing garment. If they have to start from your underwear, they can only take your book so far within the time and budget you have.

Putting on your own clothes, in this case, takes hard work. Authors often say they spent more time revising than they did writing their initial draft. But if you skip this stage, your book will not be the best it could be.

In this guide, I'll walk you through an extensive self-editing process that includes multiple read-throughs. By adopting this process, you'll lessen the load of your editor—which *saves you money*—but more importantly, you'll

- end up with a better book
- challenge your writing brain
- learn your writing weaknesses

So while you technically can skip the self-editing, you really don't want to. And while AI can help you (I used it in my own self-editing for this book to flag wordy and unclear sentences and check for clarity), you still need to understand the basic principles of self-editing to guide any AI tool effectively. And even then, you shouldn't use just AI. Editing still requires a lot of human effort.

So long story short? The stronger your manuscript is when your editor gets it, the better your published book will be and the less money you'll spend on professional editing.

If you want more guided self-editing, check out my Manuscript Checkup services. I'll professionally edit your first 10k words and provide a one-on-one coaching call to teach you how to edit for the topics your manuscript needs most. After the call, I provide feedback on one self-edited chapter to help you apply the techniques with confidence (for more information, see appendix A).

Why do I need to hire an editor after thorough self-editing?

Self-editing is important, but self-editing alone won't bring your manuscript to its full potential. Even trained professional editors hire editors. I'm paying someone to edit mine. I know, I know. That's probably not what you wanted to hear. "Come on, Katie, after I do all this work myself, I still have to go hire someone?"

But you can never see your book from the reader's perspective because you wrote it so know too much. Now you need a pro who can provide that outside view. Plus, a good editor has undergone editorial training. You haven't (and no, this book doesn't qualify you as a professional editor).

If hiring a professional editor is not an option for you right now, though, don't let that stop you from pursuing your dream. You can go through this self-editing process more than once and enlist several beta readers to help strengthen your work. And if you publish without a professional edit, you can always invest your initial profits into hiring an editor down the road to revise and republish an updated second edition.

Preparing to self-edit

Before you begin this self-editing process, make sure you've got some distance from your manuscript. Wait a few weeks, or even months if needed, after you finish writing. Fresh eyes catch what tired ones miss.

Some writers like to read through their manuscript once and take notes before beginning their edits. Others dive straight in. Both work—pick whichever matches your brain.

> ### PAUSE HERE
>
> If you don't have enough distance from your first draft, put this book down and come back to it later.
>
> If you do have distance and you'd like to read through your manuscript before editing it, pause and do that now, then come back to this book to start the self-editing process.

How this guide is structured

This guide is designed to be used selectively, as a toolbox, not a linear nonfiction book. You'll get the most value by choosing to read what you need, when you need it.

EDITING PASSES

I've broken the self-editing process into four internal passes—story, scene, writing, and technical—plus an optional feedback pass.

Complete the four internal passes in order. After each one, you'll see a "stop here" page. Stop there, do that pass on your manuscript, then move to the next one.

> If the idea of multiple passes overwhelms you, you have options:
>
> First, consider reading or skimming only what you need for your chosen topics—each editing checklist will guide you to the specific sections or elements you need to review.
>
> Alternatively, you could focus on just the story and writing passes to get the most bang for your buck and skip the scene and technical passes. Get those quick wins first. Then hand it over to your editor without doing those other passes.
>
> Yes, completing all four passes will give you the best results. But I don't want to overwhelm you if this is your first foray into self-editing.

Then you have the feedback pass, which still belongs in the self-editing process but differs from the internal passes because it introduces outside perspectives, beta readers and critique partners. With this pass, you don't need to go through your whole manuscript—just the areas your readers flagged.

You have two good options for when to do the feedback pass:

- After the story and scene passes: Do your big-picture revision first (story + scene), then get critique partner and/or beta reader feedback, and come back to the writing and technical passes afterward.
- After all four internal passes: Do the story, scene, writing, and technical passes on your own, then get outside feedback on a more polished draft.

If you chose the first option, then jump to the feedback pass after the scene pass.

Don't go wild like I did! I had my beta readers giving me feedback at the same time I was self-editing this book. Long story about why it played out that way. But that meant my beta readers just ended up giving feedback on things I had already noticed and fixed.

EDITING TOPICS

Don't try to address every topic in a single pass. Instead, focus on *two or three* editing topics in each pass that you know are weak spots for you—either ones you've noticed or ones others have pointed out. For example, when doing your one or two story passes, you might choose to edit for plot structure, plot continuity, and believable characters, not all eight topics.

To help with picking your editing priorities, I'm currently developing a manuscript diagnostic tool designed to work alongside this guide. The tool is intended to help you identify which editing topics are most important for your specific manuscript, along with a small number of example revisions in my editing style, so you can focus your revision time where it will matter most (see appendix A for more information).

SELF-EDITING IN PRACTICE

Each editing topic includes a practice section. Before you read my revision, try editing the example yourself. (I revised each example to address only that specific editing topic, leaving other potential issues unchanged.)

Note: The self-editing in practice sections come from various sources:

- My original examples
- AI-generated examples from ChatGPT or Claude (always noted)
- Anonymized examples from previous clients' manuscripts, used with permission

After the practice section, each topic includes a checklist you can use to revise your manuscript for that topic. You'll also find the master checklist in appendix C.

PERSONALIZED WORKBOOK

You can create a customized workbook for each pass that includes only the self-editing in practice exercises and editing steps for your chosen topics. This way, you can practice editing those passages in a Word document or print them out and edit by hand. Then use your customized checklist to apply the concepts to your manuscript.

At the start of each pass or "stop here" page, use the link or QR code to select your topics and generate a custom workbook for that pass.

A QUICK NOTE ABOUT REPETITION

Because you'll be choosing your own path through this guide—selecting different topics in each editing pass—you may see certain concepts appear in more than one topic. That overlap is intentional; many skills naturally connect. So I repeat definitions and briefly re-explain a concept when that overlap occurs. At times, I direct you to where the full lesson is so I don't reteach the concept completely.

1. Pick two or three topics in each pass.

2. Read those editing topics and do the self-editing in practice exercises (you practice first, then check my revision).

3. Use the checklists to revise your manuscript for those two or three topics in one or two passes.

4. Move on to the next pass and repeat.

ADDITIONAL RESOURCES

If you're looking for resources on your entire journey, check both appendices. Appendix A contains resources I created to help you with your self-editing, and appendix B includes some of my favorite author communities, book marketing programs, audiobook narration resources, courses, and recommended reading—basically a toolbox to help you with your entire journey.

Now remember: Self-editing is the beginning, not the end. Once you complete the work in this book, you still need to work with a professional editor.

But I'm going to help you do it. I'm gifting you The Professional Editing Roadmap. This free six-part email course walks you through every step of what comes next, from understanding the levels of editing and budgeting for them, to finding the right editor and knowing what to expect when you work together, to understanding how to implement their feedback.

Get it free at http://beaconpointservices.org/get-free-resource/. Check out the Gift for You page after the conclusion for a QR code and more information.

STORY PASS

First things first:

If you didn't intentionally select your point of view (POV), don't know what that is, or are unsure if you have the right one, skip to the "Pick the Best POV" topic. After reading that, decide whether you need to change your POV. If you do, put this book down and focus on revising your story for POV before you read any further. It won't be worth it to edit for anything else if you don't first have the best POV for your story. So if you need to, skip to that topic now and then come back to read the rest of this page.

Okay, at this point, either you don't need to check for POV, or you've already revised it. Either way, you're ready for the rest of the story pass.

Rest of the story pass:

Even though sentence-level issues are easier to spot, story must come first. Let's follow Maria's advice from *The Sound of Music* and start at the beginning. Story is that beginning because there's no point in polishing scenes or sentences if the foundation is shaky.

A solid foundation requires three forces, which drive every story: what your protagonist is trying to accomplish (goal), why it matters to them (motivation), and what's blocking their path (conflict). These three elements in turn influence the two arcs that define your story: plot (the external journey from point A to point B) and character (the internal transformation along the way).

Your characters drive your plot through their choices and actions, while your plot reveals your characters through the obstacles they face.

So, this self-editing pass requires you to track both character arcs and plot threads throughout the entire manuscript, so you'll want to read through your whole book.

> ### Scene versus story
>
> While some of the editing steps in the story pass ask you to check individual scenes, I approach the topic as a whole at the story level, not the scene level. But to complete the tasks, you'll need to know what a scene is.
>
> ### What's a scene?
>
> A unit of action, unfolding in continuous time, with its own mini-story arc and a clear beginning, middle, and end. When you make a significant jump in time or location or shift character focus, you start a new scene.

Remember, choose just two to three topics (in addition to the POV topic, if you needed that one) to read and apply in this pass, focusing on the ones your story needs most.

I'm also developing a manuscript diagnostic tool designed to help authors pinpoint their highest-priority editing topics more quickly and accurately, using an editorial eye rather than an author's eye. If you'd like to learn more about this upcoming resource or sign up to get notified when it's ready, see appendix A. In the meantime, I offer a Manuscript Checkup service, providing personalized guidance to help you decide what to self-edit for (see appendix A to learn more about both options).

But in general, if your story struggles with . . .

Pacing, saggy middle, or a plot that feels aimless:

- Follow a plot structure (page 23)
- Create cause-and-effect chains (page 44)

- Establish and escalate your story's central conflict (page 36)

Plot holes, contradictions, or "that doesn't make sense" feedback:

- Ensure plot continuity (page 51)
- Organize the timeline effectively (page 58)

A flat main character readers don't care about:

- Make characters believable (page 65)
- Ensure characters are dynamic (page 80)

Side characters who are flat or caricatures or who overshadow the main character:

- Create good secondary characters (page 89)

Personalized workbook: To generate your customizable story pass workbook, scan the QR code or visit https://beaconpointservices.org/generate-fiction-personalized-workbook.

For best results, open on a computer or tablet to download and edit the Word document.

Complexity note

Story-level issues are often the hardest to self-edit because plot and character problems can be difficult to see; they require you to look at the whole story at once. Since I can't include an entire manuscript here, it was a little harder to provide self-editing in practice exercises. But hopefully, the practices I have provided will help you track patterns and connections across your draft.

Point of View

Pick the Best Point of View

Your point of view (POV) shapes everything, from the intimacy readers feel with your characters to how tension unfolds on the page. That's why it's so important to get it right. But whether you picked your POV or it evolved while you were writing, it may not be serving your story as well as it could. Before you can evaluate whether you have the best POV for your story, let's clarify what it is and what options you can choose from.

Point of view basics

POV is the lens through which your reader experiences your story. You really only need to worry about three choices: first person, third person, or omniscient. Yes, variations of those exist, but those three carry 99 percent of what most writers need. Let me walk you through them in order of "zoom level."

Narrative distance overlap

In this topic, I'll only discuss narrative distance at the conceptual level because POV determines your story's default distance. For practical techniques on closing or widening distance, see the "Deepen Interiority and Close Narrative Distance" topic in the writing pass.

Omniscient: Think of this as a drone camera: high up, seeing every-thing. The narrator can dip into anyone's head, jump across time, and reveal information no single character would know. This POV is powerful but also the trickiest to pull off because it creates the widest distance between the reader and the characters. Unless you feel confident and understand omniscient well, don't use this POV.

> "No one thought about the recent departure of Mia and Pearl from the house on Winslow Road" (*Little Fires Everywhere* by Celeste Ng).

Third person: This is your flexible middle ground. You stick to one character's lens ("she," "he," "they"), but you control how close the reader gets. You can slide between a more neutral overview and deep, intimate access. It's the most commonly used POV for good reason: It adapts to almost any story.

> "Fern came slowly down the stairs. Her eyes were red from crying" (*Charlotte's Web* by E.B. White).

First person: This is the closest POV. The narrator is the character ("I"), so everything is filtered through their voice, biases, and emotional world.

> "I fell in love the way you fall asleep: slowly, then all at once" (*The Fault in Our Stars* by John Green).

With both first person and third person, you can have a single POV character or multiple POV characters. If you opt for multiple, however, you have to stick to one character per scene or chapter.

***

While you've already written your story at this stage, you may not have landed on the best POV yet, and changing your POV can require deep revision. This is why I had you start here. Notice I said "best," not "right." Choose the POV that best reveals your story and themes. Use the following tools to evaluate whether the one you're using best serves your story.

Tool 1: Pros and cons

I love a good pro-and-con list when making a decision (marrying my husband might've been the only time I didn't make one). This breakdown can help you evaluate your options.

First person pros:

- You can invite the reader into the POV character's world, fostering a deep connection.
- You can engage and captivate the reader more with a unique character voice rather than a neutral voice.
- You can potentially create more suspense, as the reader will be in the dark about anything the narrator doesn't know.
- You can more easily show the narrator's motivations and internal conflicts.

First-person cons:

- You can't include information the POV character wouldn't know.
- You may struggle to portray other characters, as everything must be filtered through the POV character's perspective.

To use first person well, your POV character (or characters) must be interesting enough with a strong enough voice that a reader isn't bored.

Third-person pros:

- You can play more with narrative distance, bringing the reader more intimately into the character's world (deep third) or keeping a wider distance (limited third).
- You have the flexibility to use a more neutral narrator tone at certain times and a more intimate character voice at other times.
- You can potentially create more suspense, as the reader will be in the dark about anything the narrator doesn't know.

Third-person cons:

- You can't include information the POV character wouldn't know.
- You do sacrifice a bit of intimacy, as the use of the character's name and "she," "he," "they" reminds the reader they're being told a story.

As mentioned, third person exists on a continuum. With third person, you can use a distant, limited third, which allows for some narrative "explaining" and a more neutral voice, and then pick key moments to go into deep third. We'll explore this more in "Deepen Interiority and Close the Narrative Distance."

Omniscient pros:

- You can give information about multiple characters in a given scene.
- You can play with dramatic irony (the narrator knows things characters don't).

Omniscient cons:

- You have to maintain a wider distance between the character and the reader.
- You may struggle to write this POV in a way that avoids mental whiplash and reader disorientation.

Omniscient is the hardest POV to write, and I don't recommend it for newer writers.

Tool 2: Guiding questions

If you're torn between POV options, these questions will point you in the right direction. Don't overthink them—just answer honestly as the storyteller you already are.

1. How intimate do you want the reader to be with the character(s)? As mentioned, first person and deep third will give you the most intimacy, followed by limited third and then omniscient.

2. Do you want a unified, specific voice, or would you like to have more flexibility with voice? In first person, voice is everything. Your narrator's personality, speech patterns, and worldview should shine through every sentence. If your first-person narrative sounds generic or could belong to anyone, you're not leveraging the POV's strength.

   In third person, you have more flexibility with voice because you're not locked into one character's exact speaking style. The voice can be more neutral at times or carry more flavor at other times. This can be freeing if maintaining a distinct first-person voice for an entire novel feels constraining.

3. What information does the reader need access to? If you keep forcing your protagonist to overhear conversations or witness events just to deliver information to the reader, you should either consider switching POV or trust the story enough to let key moments happen off-page.

Tool 3: Red flags

These red flags may indicate your POV isn't serving your story.

1. It's unclear who's narrating. If beta readers get confused about whose head they're in, your POV characters might be too similar, or you might be head hopping unintentionally.
2. The story feels lifeless despite a good plot and characters. A mismatch between the story and the POV drains the page of energy. A tense thriller told in a distant, omniscient voice might lack urgency. An intimate first-person character study might feel claustrophobic if the narrator isn't compelling.
3. You're explaining things the POV character wouldn't think about. If you're in close third or first person but find yourself including information the character wouldn't naturally consider, you're either info dumping or you need omniscient narration.

Tool 4: Rewrite test

If you suspect your POV isn't working, try this exercise:

> Select a key scene and rewrite it in a different POV. Not a different character, just a different POV. So if you've written in first person, try third or omniscient. Truly reimagine how that scene would unfold from another perspective or at a different distance.

Often, one version will feel more alive right away. Trust that instinct. Sometimes the "right" POV makes everything click into place—pacing improves, voice strengthens, and the story finds its natural rhythm.

Using multiple POV characters

If you're writing in first person or third person, you can use multiple POV characters. So if you go with either of those options, choose which characters will be POV characters. Keep in mind: The "less is more" adage applies here.

Look at every character who gets a POV scene:

- Do they appear in the climactic moment of your story?
- Do they contribute unique information throughout the narrative?
- Are they present at regular intervals, or do they pop up randomly?

Authors will often make a character a POV character simply because it's convenient for a particular scene. But if that character only narrates once or twice, their presence disrupts the story's cohesion. If that's the case with one of your characters, ask, Is there a way to convey this information through my main POV character(s)? If not, is it essential information?

Another common mistake is using a POV character because you think the reader needs more information than they actually do. For example, some thrillers include chapters in the villain's POV. While this can work well in some cases, it can also give too much away. In a thriller I edited, I suggested the author cut the chapters told from the villain's POV because it actually increased tension when the reader didn't know the villain's thought process or next move before it happened.

Deciding to change

I won't sugarcoat it: Changing POV mid-revision is no small task. It's not a "quick search-and-replace" situation. But if your current POV is holding your story back, the extra work pays off in a big way. Many published authors have rewritten entire drafts after realizing their POV was working against them, and the transformation is almost always worth it.

> **No self-editing in practice exercises**
>
> This topic differs from the others because it doesn't include a self-editing in practice section. It would be hard to determine from a short passage if the story would be better served from a different POV.

EDITING STEPS

- ❏ Identify the current POV: omniscient, first, or third.
- ❏ Reread three important scenes (including your climax and a turning point) and assess them for all the POV considerations:
  - Does the current POV create the emotional impact you intended? If not, consider a POV with deeper intimacy.
  - Do the scenes feel constricted by a specific character's voice? If so, consider using third person instead of first.
  - Is your current POV forcing you to use contrived situations (overheard conversations, convenient observations, flashbacks) to convey information? If so, consider using a different POV entirely or a different POV character. You can also delete those situations entirely and let them happen off-page.
- ❏ Check for red flags that may signal POV mismatch (either different POV or different POV characters).
  - Frequent head hopping or unclear viewpoint
  - Explanations the POV character wouldn't naturally think
  - Overexplaining or awkward justification for giving the reader information
  - Disorientation caused by switching too often between characters
- ❏ Run the rewrite test. Choose one pivotal scene and rewrite it in a different POV (first, third, or omniscient).
  - Which version feels more alive?
  - Which version reveals tension, emotion, and characterization more effectively?
  - Which version aligns better with the themes or tone you're aiming for?
- ❏ If you have multiple POV characters, list every character who has a POV scene. Mark how often they appear as a narrator. If someone has fewer than three scenes as a POV character or if long stretches pass between their appearances, strongly reconsider whether they're truly necessary as a POV character.

❑ Make the POV decision and any necessary revisions to comply with it:
- Which POV will you use (current POV or a different one)?
- What characters will be POV characters?

Plot

Follow a Plot Structure

Yes, I'm starting with plot structure, the order in which the plot unfolds. I can feel some of you rolling your eyes, ready to close this book because you don't want an unoriginal, formulaic story. I don't want you to write that either. These frameworks exist to diagnose story problems, not to make your writing formulaic.

Every story has a structure. That's simply the truth. But you get to create what goes into that structure and how to best use it. You can also switch the order of some plot points, but not the key plot points that need to happen in specific spots for your story to work. So, yes, you have creative control, but you should still anchor your story in an established framework to ensure you have a solid structure.

Dozens of plot frameworks exist: three-act structure, Save the Cat, Hero's Journey, Story Circle, and so on. But don't let the list intimidate you. They all boil down to a few shared elements:

- Exposition
- Rising action
- Climax
- Falling action
- Resolution

Did that just drop you back into English class? (Raise your hand if you ever had to chart the plot points of classic literature on that plot structure chart.) Yep, these elements of story have been around forever, and yes, some of these terms sound like they belong on a high school test, but they're actually super helpful once you see them in action.

By charting your plot using a set framework, you can diagnose why your story doesn't quite work or why it has pacing issues.

Three-act structure

I can't teach you every story framework in this guide. So, to model editing for this concept, let's use the three-act structure, since all structures stem from that classic.

Act 1: The setup (first 25 percent)

- Exposition. This sets up the story and the setting, giving the reader an idea of the protagonist and their ordinary world.
- Inciting incident. This event sets the story in motion, introducing the conflict, goal, challenge, etc.
- Plot point one. Now presented with the conflict, the protagonist must engage with it in some way and make a critical choice. This choice then brings consequences, making it clear that the character can't return to their ordinary world until they achieve their goal. That main central goal propels them forward.

Act 2: Confrontation

- Rising action. The character faces some obstacles on the way to their goal, pushing them to evolve and grow. During this rising action, the central conflict becomes more complicated. This part also contains subplots that contribute to the overall tension and rising conflict.
- Midpoint. Your character either thinks they'll soon have it all wrapped up, wants to give up, or thinks they've won. But, of course, not all is as it seems. Following this midpoint, the trajectory shifts with a new, surprising revelation or plot twist, along

with increased stakes. This revelation or plot twist reveals an essential truth for the protagonist. (Note this can include more than one revelation.)

- Plot point two. With the events of the midpoint, the conflict has now escalated. The protagonist thought they'd been making headway on their goal, but whatever happened at the midpoint threw everything off. Now they're forced to make another major decision to combat the new conflicts, and, once again, they can't go back once they commit.

Act 3: Resolution (last 25 percent)

- Low point, or dark night of the soul. With renewed commitment, the protagonist is confident they'll win, but they have a false victory. For a moment, it seems like they've won, but they haven't. Maybe they got a victory of sorts but took too much damage, or maybe what they thought would work didn't at all. Either way, they feel all is lost and must search their soul for renewed strength to continue.
- Climax. The moment your story has been building toward, when your character's situation is resolved. Either the character achieved their plot goal, or it no longer makes sense for them to pursue it.
- Denouement. All subplots and loose ends are tied up.

To help you see this structure in action, I've plotted out the book *The Hate U Give* by Angie Thomas.

Exposition: Sixteen-year-old Starr Carter lives in the poor, predominantly Black neighborhood of Garden Heights but attends a wealthy, predominantly white prep school, Williamson. She code-switches between these two worlds, feeling like two different people.

Inciting incident: She witnesses her childhood friend Khalil being shot and killed by a white police officer. Khalil was unarmed.

Plot point one: Starr decides to testify anonymously before the grand jury about what she witnessed.

Rising action: Many obstacles stand in her way.

- The media vilifies Khalil, suggesting he was a drug dealer and thug.
- Her Williamson friends make insensitive comments.
- Her boyfriend, Chris, doesn't understand her world.
- King, a local gang leader, threatens her family.
- She struggles with PTSD from witnessing the shooting.

Midpoint: Starr gives her grand jury testimony, speaking truth about what happened and feeling confident she's done the right thing. However, this moment also heightens the stakes as King escalates his threats and the neighborhood awaits the grand jury's decision.

Second plot point: The grand jury decides not to indict the accused officer. Starr is devastated but decides to go public as a witness, giving a television interview and joining the protests. She can no longer hide between her two worlds. She must fully embrace her authentic self and fight injustice openly.

Dark night of the soul: During a protest, riots break out. King firebombs Starr's family's store, and many other buildings are destroyed. She feels responsible for the destruction and questions whether speaking out made anything better or just made everything worse. She doubts whether one voice can change anything.

Climax: At the riot, Starr confronts the police, standing on a car with a megaphone. When police threaten the crowd with tear gas, she faces them down. Separately, King threatens her family with a gun, but Starr's father and neighbors unite to stand against him. King is arrested. Starr realizes her voice does matter, as she's already started change by inspiring others to speak up.

Denouement: The neighborhood begins rebuilding. Starr stops code-switching and brings her whole authentic self to Williamson. She maintains her relationship with Chris, who now understands her world better. While the officer wasn't indicted, Starr has found her voice and purpose, and the community has come together. The cycle of change has begun.

Using other frameworks

The three-act structure is universal across genres, so you can use it to analyze any story. However, you may want to use a different framework, depending on your goals.

Use these other structures (a quick Google search can teach you the plot points for each one) when you

- want to focus on a character's transformation, growth, and self-discovery or to send your main character on a classic quest = Hero's Journey
- want a more detailed analysis of specific plot points to ensure all acts are well fleshed out = Save the Cat
- have a Hero's Journey but want to focus more on character growth – Dan Harmon's Story Circle
- want a looser structure = seven-point story structure

Hopefully, you see now that a set framework doesn't ruin your creativity. You still have full control over the plot; a framework just ensures you have a plot that works on a structural level.

Pacing and framework

Pacing matters a lot because moving too fast or too slowly can be a quick way to lose readers. A framework with guideposts of "this plot point happens roughly at this percent" can help analyze that pacing.

For example, in the three-act structure, act 1 should only take up the first 25 percent of your manuscript. If you find that act is way longer, tighten it up to get to the second act sooner.

If act 2 is longer than 50 percent and your second plot point happens at, say, the 85 percent point, your pacing is off, and your story most likely drags.

Self-editing in practice

Using the three-act structure as a guide, review these plot outlines and identify any potential issues.

Original A:

> Mara lived in Bellwick, a mountain town where every shop, school, and home ran according to the great clocktower in the square. Her father, the former clockmaker, had disappeared five years earlier, leaving behind only a broken silver pocket watch and a note that said, *Keep time safe.*
>
> One afternoon, the clocktower stopped, and the whole town froze. Mara was the only one who could move.
>
> She ran to the clocktower and found a boy named Theo prying open the gears. He said he was trying to stop the Time Thieves from finding the hidden gear Mara's father had protected. If they found it, they could rewrite the town's history.
>
> Mara didn't believe him, so she went home.

The next morning, everything was normal again. Nobody remembered freezing. Mara decided the whole thing must have been a dream and returned to baking.

Three days later, the Time Thieves arrived and captured Theo. They demanded that Mara give them the hidden gear.

Mara does not know what the hidden gear is. She panics. They give her one week.

She tries to find it as each day the Time Thieves add another complication to the town and her life. Eventually, she remembers her father had taught her years ago, but she had just forgotten.

She climbed the clocktower, placed the gear into the mechanism, and the Time Thieves vanished.

Everyone cheered.

Then Theo returned and explained that Mara's father was still alive, trapped in a lost hour beneath the clocktower (generated by ChatGPT).

PAUSE HERE

Open your personalized workbook on your computer and review the practice exercise, asking

- Label each event using the three-act structure framework. What's the inciting incident, plot point one, and so on?

- Which plot points arrive too early, too late, or without sufficient setup?

- Which plot points are missing or incomplete?

Now create a revised outline, labeling each plot point, before reading the actual outline provided below.

Problems with original:

The story is missing plot point one (she never makes a choice), a mid-point (Mara never learns something that changes her understanding of the conflict or shifts the story), and the dark night of the soul. Also the father-is-alive reveal comes too late. It belongs in Act 2, not after the climax.

Revised A:

> Exposition: Mara lives in Bellwick, a mountain town where every shop, school, and home runs according to the great clocktower. Her father, the former clockmaker, disappeared five years ago, leaving behind only a broken pocket watch and a note that said, *Keep time safe*. Mara works at the bakery and avoids anything connected to clocks or her father's old workshop.
>
> Inciting Incident: One afternoon, the clocktower stopped, and the whole town froze. Mara was the only one who could move. Inside the clocktower, she finds Theo, a boy trying to protect the hidden gear her father once guarded. He warns her that the Time Thieves are coming for it.
>
> Plot Point One: Mara wants to ignore the problem, but when the Time Thieves steal her father's pocket watch and freeze the bakery with her friends inside, she chooses to help Theo find the hidden gear. Now she can't return to ordinary life until she stops them.
>
> Rising Action: Mara and Theo search her father's workshop, decode old clockmaker notes, and follow clues through frozen pockets of time beneath Bellwick. She learns her father was protecting the town's timeline. Each clue brings the Time Thieves closer too.
>
> Midpoint: Mara finds the hidden gear and thinks they can fix everything. But when she touches it, she sees the truth: Her father is alive and in a lost hour to keep the Time Thieves from rewriting

Bellwick's history. Now she needs to save her father, not just the town.

Plot Point Two: The Time Thieves capture Theo and offer Mara a bargain: give them the gear, and they'll release her father. Mara refuses, choosing to protect the town first, even though it may cost her the chance to save him.

Low Point: Mara tries to repair the clocktower herself, but the gear cracks, Theo remains trapped, and the town begins disappearing street by street. For a moment, Mara believes she has failed everyone.

Climax: Mara realizes the pocket watch is the missing piece. She places both the watch and the cracked gear into the clocktower, restoring Bellwick's timeline and breaking the lost hour.

The Time Thieves vanish, Theo is freed, and her father returns.

Denouement: Bellwick returns to normal, but Mara no longer hides from her father's legacy. She reopens the bakery in the mornings and repairs clocks with her father in the afternoons, now understanding what it means to keep time safe (generated by ChatGPT).

Now we have a first plot point, where she makes a decision, a midpoint that shifts the story, and a dark night of the soul. By moving the reveal of her father earlier, we get a more satisfying arc.

Original B Outline for *The Fault in Our Stars* by John Green with structural issues added in:

Hazel Grace Lancaster has terminal thyroid cancer that has spread to her lungs. She's depressed and withdrawn. She attends a cancer support group where she meets Augustus Waters, who's in remission from osteosarcoma. They're immediately attracted to each other, bonding over books and their shared skepticism of cancer clichés. Hazel introduces Augustus to her favorite novel, *An Imperial Affliction*, which ends mid-sentence, leaving the fates of the characters unknown. Augustus reads it and becomes equally obsessed with finding out what happens to the characters.

Augustus contacts the reclusive author, Peter Van Houten, through his assistant. Van Houten invites them to Amsterdam to discuss the book's ending. Augustus uses his wish from a cancer foundation to take Hazel to Amsterdam, and her parents agree to let her go.

In Amsterdam, they visit the Anne Frank House and share their first kiss. They have dinner at an expensive restaurant, where Augustus reveals his cancer has returned and spread throughout his body. He's terminal now too. They meet Van Houten, who turns out to be a cruel drunk who refuses to answer Hazel's questions about the book and insults them both.

Back home, Augustus's health deteriorates rapidly. He organizes a pre-funeral, where his friends eulogize him while he's still alive. Shortly after, Augustus dies. At his funeral, Van Houten appears, claiming Augustus asked him to attend. Hazel later discovers Augustus wrote her a eulogy disguised as a sequel to *An Imperial Affliction*, sending it to Van Houten to edit. Van Houten returns the pages to Hazel, and she reads Augustus's final words about their love.

PAUSE HERE

- Label each event using the three-act structure framework. What's the inciting incident, plot point one, etc.?

- Which plot points arrive too early, too late, or without sufficient setup?

- Which plot points are missing or incomplete?

Now create a revised outline, labeling each plot point, before reading the actual outline provided below.

Problems with original:

The first plot point isn't fully fleshed out. It's unclear what choice Hazel had to make after the inciting incident and what goal she sets from there. The rising action is missing obstacles, and the dark night of the soul is missing entirely.

Revised B:

> Exposition: Hazel Grace Lancaster has terminal thyroid cancer that has spread to her lungs. She's depressed and withdrawn.
>
> Inciting incident: She attends a cancer support group where she meets Augustus Waters, who's in remission from osteosarcoma. They're immediately attracted to each other, bonding over books and their shared skepticism of cancer clichés.
>
> Plot point one (added the real details of the choice Hazel has to make at this juncture): Hazel introduces Augustus to her favorite novel, *An Imperial Affliction*, which ends mid-sentence. Augustus reads it and becomes equally obsessed with finding out what happens to the characters. Hazel has always avoided romantic relationships because she doesn't want to hurt people when she dies, but Augustus pursues her relentlessly. She must make a critical choice: open herself to love despite knowing she's dying or push Augustus away to protect him. She chooses to let herself fall in love with Augustus, accepting that this relationship will cause pain but deciding it's worth it.
>
> Rising action (added in the real obstacles): Augustus contacts the reclusive author, Peter Van Houten, through his assistant. Van Houten invites them to Amsterdam to discuss the book's ending. Hazel's mother initially worries she's not healthy enough for the trip. Her doctor eventually clears her but warns about the risks. Hazel struggles with guilt over using Augustus's wish on her

obsession with the book. On the plane, Hazel has trouble breathing and needs extra oxygen, reminding them both of her fragility. In Amsterdam, they navigate the physical challenges of Hazel's oxygen tank while sightseeing.

Midpoint: At dinner, Augustus reveals his cancer has returned and spread throughout his body. He's now terminal too. They meet Van Houten, who turns out to be a cruel drunk who refuses to answer Hazel's questions about the book and insults them both.

Plot point two: Hazel realizes the answers she's been seeking don't exist, and she must decide what matters now. She commits to making Augustus's remaining time meaningful, to being present with him rather than seeking external validation or closure. She chooses love and presence over the abstract comfort of knowing a fictional ending.

Dark night of the soul (added in): Back home, Augustus's health deteriorates rapidly. Hazel watches him suffer through humiliating physical degradation: He can't control his body, he's in constant pain, and he's losing himself. One night, Augustus calls Hazel in crisis from a gas station, unable to get back in his car, covered in his own vomit. Hazel finds him in this degraded state. This is her darkest moment, seeing the person she loves reduced to helplessness, realizing that death isn't noble or beautiful but ugly and cruel. She questions whether love is worth this agony, whether she can endure watching him die. She must find the strength to stay present through his final days rather than emotionally retreat.

Climax: Augustus organizes a pre-funeral, where his friends eulogize him while he's still alive. Hazel delivers her eulogy, telling Augustus that she's grateful for their "little infinity" together and that she wouldn't trade their time for anything. (This is the emotional payout of the decision she made in plot point one.) Shortly after, Augustus dies.

Denouement: At Augustus's funeral, Van Houten appears, claiming Augustus asked him to attend. Hazel later discovers Augustus wrote her a eulogy disguised as a sequel to *An Imperial Affliction*, sending it to Van Houten to edit. Van Houten returns the pages to Hazel, and she reads Augustus's final words about their love.

Added in the decision Hazel had to make in plot point one, obstacles during the rising action, and the dark night of the soul.

EDITING STEPS

❑ Choose a framework (three-act structure, Hero's Journey, Story Circle, etc.) to guide your analysis.

❑ Outline your story's plot using your chosen framework, labeling each major plot point with its intended part of the structure (this helps you see whether your story aligns with the framework).

❑ Analyze your story for the structure:

- Do any major plot points occur too early or too late in the story?
- Are any essential plot points missing or not fully fleshed out?
- Do any plot points last too long?

❑ Delete or revise plot points that don't match the structure.

❑ Add in any missing plot points.

❑ Shorten plot points that are too long and lengthen any that are too short (a lot of the "how" to do this is covered in the writing pass, as this often comes down to the word and sentence level).

Establish and Escalate Your Story's Central Conflict

Every story needs a central conflict, the primary obstacle standing between your protagonist and what they want. This is the engine that drives your entire narrative forward. Without a clear, compelling central conflict, you don't have a story; you just have a series of events. Your central conflict should answer: What's the main problem your protagonist must solve or overcome?

You might notice I also include a conflict topic in the scene pass. Since conflict drives story, it happens at both the story and the scene levels. At this stage, you're evaluating the central story-level conflict across the manuscript, not mini-conflicts that occur within individual scenes.

Types of story-level conflict

Your story needs one clear central conflict, the main force working against your protagonist. This conflict can take different shapes, and the strongest stories combine more than one type.

External conflict: The protagonist faces opposition from outside forces—an antagonist, society, nature, or circumstance. This is the plot-level conflict readers can see and follow.

In *The Hunger Games*, Katniss must survive the Games themselves (external conflict with the Capitol and other tributes).

You can have different types of external conflicts:

- Character versus character—Harry Potter versus Voldemort (*Harry Potter*)
- Character versus society—Katniss versus the Capitol (*The Hunger Games*)
- Character versus nature—Mark versus Mars's environment (*The Martian*)
- Character versus technology—Dave Bowman versus Hal 9000, the ship's AI (*2001: A Space Odyssey*)
- Character versus supernatural—Percy Jackson versus monsters, Gods, mythological forces (*Percy Jackson*)

Internal conflict: The protagonist struggles with their own beliefs, fears, desires, or identity. This is the character-level conflict that creates emotional depth.

> Katniss also struggles with her desire to protect those she loves versus her instinct for self-preservation and her confusion about her feelings for Peeta versus Gale.

The best stories layer both external and internal conflict. Your story's external conflict provides structure and momentum, while the internal conflict provides emotional stakes and character growth. Ideally, these two conflicts are related: The external challenge forces the protagonist to confront their internal struggle.

While your story should have both types of conflict, your genre dictates whether you place more emphasis on one over the other. Many action stories or thrillers focus on the external. The internal is there, but it's not the focus, whereas with romance, the opposite is true.

Establishing your central conflict

Your central conflict should be introduced in act 1, ideally within the first few chapters. Readers need to understand three things relatively early on:

- What the protagonist wants or needs (their central goal)
- What's standing in their way (the central conflict)
- Why it matters (the stakes, the character's motivation)

This doesn't mean you reveal everything immediately, but readers should grasp the basic shape of the story's main problem. If a reader finishes your first fifty pages and can't articulate what your story is fundamentally about, your central conflict isn't clear enough.

Example:

> In the opening chapters, seventeen-year-old Maren discovers she has the rare ability to read memories stored in objects. She wants to use this gift to find her mother, who disappeared years ago. We follow her as she practices her ability, learns its limits, and sets off on her journey.

Maren is compelling, but nothing stands in her way. The central conflict hasn't been established and should be in the opening chapters.

Escalating the conflict

A static conflict becomes boring. Your central conflict should intensify as the story progresses. This happens by:

- Rising complications. Your protagonist attempts to solve the problem, which creates new obstacles or reveals that the problem is bigger than they thought.
- Increasing stakes. What your protagonist stands to lose should grow more significant as the story continues.

- Narrowing options. Your protagonist should have fewer choices and less time as they approach the climax.
- Deepening internal conflict. As external pressure increases, your protagonist's internal struggle intensifies, and they're forced to confront harder truths about themselves.

Example:

In *Breaking Bad*, Walter White initially just wants to make enough money for his family before he dies of cancer. This is his goal and the reason he started selling drugs. But the conflict of worrying about providing for his family escalates through several rising complications (he ends up having to kill in self-defense in his first cook, more dangerous people come into his life, etc.).

The stakes also increase. Initially, failure just meant his family would struggle after he was gone. But by mid-series, failure means his family gets killed by cartel violence. By the end, failure means his family is destroyed emotionally and financially, his brother-in-law is dead because of him, and he's lost everything that originally motivated him.

His options also get narrower. In season 1, Walter could have accepted help from his wealthy former business partners; pride prevented him from doing so, but the option existed. By season 5, he's burned every bridge and made enemies of everyone, and his cancer has returned. He's out of allies and time. The walls have closed in completely.

This show's also a master at deepening the internal conflict. Initially, Walter tells himself he's doing this for his family—it's a noble lie he can live with. As the series progresses, he's forced to confront that he's doing it for himself, for the power and validation he never had as a high school chemistry teacher.

Common problems

Maybe your story has a clear central conflict right at the start; maybe it doesn't. If it doesn't, well, then start there. If it does, ensure you don't have any of the other common problems I see:

- The character keeps facing the same type of obstacle without the stakes rising or the situation changing in a meaningful way.
- The main problem is solved before the story reaches its emotional or narrative peak, so the ending loses momentum.
- New problems appear that don't connect to the central question of the story, causing the narrative to feel scattered.
- The story stops building pressure, as scenes maintain the same emotional intensity instead of escalating.
- The character cares about the outcome, but the consequences don't deeply affect their identity, relationships, or values.

Self-editing in practice

Original A:

> In the opening chapters, Joel, a mid-level architect, learns that the firm he works for has been fraudulently taking credit for designs that aren't theirs, including one of his. We follow him as he goes about his workdays, quietly unsettled by what he knows. He's a sympathetic character, and the fraudulent firm is clearly corrupt, but Joel hasn't decided what he wants to do about it yet. He attends meetings, does his work, and thinks about the situation.

PAUSE HERE

Open your personalized workbook on your computer and review the practice exercise, asking

- What is standing in the main character's way?

- What is at stake for the main character?

After answering, check my revision.

Problems with original A:

Nothing is really standing in the character's way and nothing is at stake. While these opening chapters have a conflict, it's not the central conflict (the main thing standing in the character's way).

Revised A:

> Add a central conflict in the beginning chapters: Joel decides to expose them. But when he raises concerns internally, his boss makes it clear that employees who cause problems don't last long, and Joel's wife is seven months pregnant and they just bought a house. This job is the only thing keeping them afloat.

Now we have what's standing in his way and what's at stake for him.

Original B:

> Let's say we have a thriller where the protagonist is trying to find her missing sister. Early on, she faces resistance from the police. Midway through, she's threatened by a suspicious neighbor. Near the climax, she's chased by someone in a parking garage.

> ## PAUSE HERE
>
> Open your personalized workbook on your computer and review the practice exercise, asking
>
> - What common problem does this conflict progression show?
> - How would you fix it?
>
> After answering, check my revision.

Problems with original B:

The conflict presents new obstacles, but nothing is really escalating.

Revision ideas B:

- Act 1. Police dismiss her concerns (low stakes: frustration, wasted time)
- Beginning of act 2. She discovers evidence the police ignored and realizes her sister might have been involved in something dangerous (medium stakes: Her sister might have been complicit, not just a victim; the protagonist herself might be in real danger)
- End of act 2. The people involved in her sister's disappearance realize she's investigating and threaten her family (high stakes: Now she also needs to protect everyone she loves)
- Act 3: She discovers her sister is alive but trapped in a situation where a rescue attempt could get them both killed. The traffickers have made it clear that if she involves the police, her sister dies (highest stakes: She must choose between the safe option that abandons her sister and the dangerous option that might cost both their lives)

Notice how each stage reveals the problem is bigger than previously understood and what the protagonist stands to lose grows more devastating.

EDITING STEPS

❏ Identify your central conflict in one sentence: "The protagonist wants *X*, but *Y* stands in the way, and if they fail, *Z* happens." If you can't articulate this clearly, neither can your reader, and you need to go back and clarify your central conflict.

❏ Is your central conflict clear within the first few chapters? If not, cut out some of the fluff before the conflict or move the conflict earlier.

❏ Does your central conflict resolve at or very near the climax, or does it fizzle out earlier?

❏ List your major plot complications and check them for effectiveness:
  - Are your rising complications all tied to the central conflict, or do they feel unrelated?
  - Are the stakes higher in act 3 than they were in act 1?
  - Does the protagonist face a harder choice at the climax than at the inciting incident?
  - Does the final confrontation (external and/or internal) feel like the ultimate test?
  - Do the stakes feel personal or too generic?

❏ If you answered no to any of the above, revise to strengthen the escalation.

Create Cause-and-Effect Chains

Everyone, at some point, has experienced the annoyance of half the bulbs on a string of Christmas lights not turning on. Oh man, the frustration. You have to find where the connection is breaking, or buy a whole new string. But often, as long as you have the patience to find the breaking point, you can fix it. Like those lights, plot events should affect each other rather than being a random string of events. Essentially, each major event should trigger the next.

Think of cause and effect as the connective tissue of your narrative. Conflict is the spine holding the story upright and keeping it from collapsing, the central plot points form the bones, and cause-and-effect chains are what connect them. Without this connective tissue, scenes feel disconnected or pacing drags. Drafts fall flat when things simply happen without causing anything.

Your protagonist's choices should drive the story so events unfold *because* of the character, not *to* the character. If you can remove those choices from a scene and nothing changes—or if events could be rearranged without affecting anything—your cause-and-effect chain needs strengthening. Even though cause and effect shows up moment by moment at the scene level, a weak causal chain is really a story-level issue. If those connections aren't there, the whole narrative starts to wobble.

Your inciting incident happens because something disrupted your character's world.

Your rising action exists because your character takes steps (or avoids taking steps) that escalate the problem.

Your midpoint twist hits because an earlier choice or mistake finally catches up to them.

Your climax exists because every cause-and-effect domino leading up to it finally topples.

Here, you'll trace cause and effect across the story as a whole, not revise scene mechanics yet.

The chain test

To test your causal thread, list your major plot points in order. For each one, ask two questions:

- What caused this event?
- What's the effect of this event?

If you can say, "This happens because that happened," you're in excellent shape. If you hit a moment where you can't explain the chain without using words like "coincidence," "it just worked out," or "I needed something dramatic here," that's your red flag.

Original:

> There's a stampede in a gorge. King Mufasa dies, and Scar takes over. His son, Simba, wanders into a jungle. He meets Timon and Pumbaa and has a good time. Years pass. The Pride Lands are dry and struggling. Nala appears in the jungle. Simba goes back home and becomes king.

> *I'm sure you recognize this as the plot of The Lion King. All the events are in order, but in this version, nothing causes the next event. These events just happen.*

Revised:

> The stampede happens inside a gorge with no escape routes, which is what makes Mufasa's rescue attempt fatal. Scar convinces Simba he caused his father's death, which drives him to flee in shame. Since the Pride Lands doesn't have a rightful ruler, Scar can seize power unchallenged. Scar's rule is exploitative rather than balanced, which is what causes the Pride Lands to become barren and overhunted. The food scarcity is what forces Nala to venture far enough from home to find Simba, and she forces him to confront what he ran from. Rafiki shows him his father's spirit, which breaks through his denial and compels him to return.
>
> *In the real version, each situation produces conditions or a character does something that makes the next event not just possible but inevitable.*

If you find some plot points just sit next to each other and one doesn't cause the other (either the situation or the character's choices in that plot event), then you may need to make a tough choice. You might realize a scene—or even a whole chapter—exists only because you wanted your character to experience something cool or intense, even though nothing in the story warranted it. In that case, the scene needs to go or be reworked so it naturally grows out of the character's actions. Either way, you need to ensure your plot happens *because* of your characters, not just *to* them. A strong causal chain transforms your story from a list of events into a narrative that feels inevitable, meaningful, and deeply satisfying.

Original:

> In act two of a fantasy novel, the protagonist Kael has just escaped a prison cell after bribing a guard with a stolen gemstone. Two chapters later, Kael is in a black market bazaar, where he gets into a fight with a weapons dealer and steals a rare blade (generated by Claude).

Nothing about the escape caused the bazaar scene to happen.

Revised 1:

> If the stolen blade doesn't pay off later in the story, the bazaar scene is just an action set piece. Cut it. The escape scene alone moves Kael forward. Adding an unconnected scene after it actually dilutes the momentum of the escape rather than building on it.

Revised 2:

> When Kael bribes the guard, he uses the only gemstone he had, the one he was going to use to pay his contact in the black market. Now he arrives at the bazaar empty-handed, and his contact refuses to help him. Desperate, Kael spots a rare blade on a dealer's table, one he knows his contact will accept as payment, and steals it. The fight breaks out when the dealer catches him.

Now this scene happens because of the events in the last one, so it can stay.

Self-editing in practice

Original A:

> In one chapter, Evan wakes up late for work and rushes out the door. At the office, his boss announces a surprise inspection from corporate, which puts everyone on edge. Later that night, Evan goes to a bar with his friend, where they get into a heated argument about politics. The next morning, Evan receives a mysterious letter in the mail warning him not to trust anyone (generated by ChatGPT).

PAUSE HERE

Open your personalized workbook on your computer and review the practice exercise, asking

- Do the events feel linked or disconnected?
- Can you identify a clear "this happens *because* that happened"?
- Does any scene feel like a detour rather than a natural consequence?

After answering, create a revised scene summary before reading mine.

Problem with original:

While these events all seem interesting, they don't build on each other.

Revised A:

> Evan wakes up late for work, and in his rush, he forgets the quarterly financial reports on his kitchen counter. When corporate shows up for the surprise inspection, the missing reports make

Evan look incompetent, and his boss tears into him in front of the whole office. Humiliated and angry, Evan goes to a bar that night to blow off steam with his friend, but when his friend points out that Evan might lose his job, the conversation spirals into an argument. The next morning, Evan finds a mysterious letter in his mailbox. It says, "We know you're desperate. Meet us tonight, and we'll help you keep your job. But don't trust anyone."

Even though the events remained nearly the same, the added clarity of causality strengthened them.

Original B:

Mara discovers an old key in her grandmother's attic. Excited, she spends hours trying it on different locked boxes and drawers around the house. Later, she goes to a town festival with her friends, where they play games, eat funnel cakes, and watch the fireworks. The next morning, she sneaks back into the attic and finds a trunk that the key finally opens—inside is a stack of letters revealing a long-hidden family secret.

PAUSE HERE

- Do the events feel linked or disconnected?
- Can you identify a clear "this happens *because* that happened"?
- Does any scene feel like a detour rather than a natural consequence?

After answering, create a revised scene summary before reading mine.

Problems with original:

Most of the events show clear cause and effect, but the festival doesn't connect to anything. You can delete it, but suppose the festival scene highlights the character's personality and her dynamic with her friends—elements that play a pivotal role in the plot. In that case, you would need to add a causal thread.

Revised B (two ideas):

- Delete the scene at the town festival and pick a different scene to showcase Mara's personality and relationship with her friends
- Add that when Mara searches the house's drawers, she finds a note about a special "festival box" kept at the town fair each year. So while at the festival with her friends, she's looking for clues. She doesn't find anything, but the next morning, when she finds the stack of letters, she uncovers the family secret along with clues about where to find the box and what it's for. Now the scene has a causal relationship, as well as revealing her character and her relationship with friends.

EDITING STEPS

❑ Ask cause-and-effect questions for each scene: What caused this event, and what effect does this event have on the story or character?

❑ If a scene doesn't follow a causal thread, revise or delete.

- If the scene can advance the plot, reveal character, or show relationships, consider keeping it and strengthening the causal link or deleting it and showing the advancement and characterization in a different scene.
- If it doesn't reveal character or show relationships, delete it.

Ensure Plot Continuity

Readers love to play "spot the plot hole," and this shows up in their book reviews. A plot hole can crop up in several ways: contradictory events, unexplained events, illogical or unlikely events, impossible events, and/or unresolved storylines.

- Contradictory events = A character is tall enough to reach the top shelf but then later uses a ladder to reach that same shelf.
- Unexplained events = A character finds a hidden treasure in their attic, and we never learn how it got there.
- Illogical or unlikely events = A never-before-defeated villain is defeated in combat by someone without any training, without a clear explanation.
- Impossible events = A character can see what's going on inside their neighbor's house even though it's dark outside and the lights are turned off.
- Unresolved events = A character promised to help their friend with their homework but never does, and the reader is never told why.

Yep, plot holes are so sneaky. Beta readers will uncover some of them for you before you hire an editor, but you can weed some out yourself even before the beta reading phase. To do so, though, you must step away from your manuscript for a while so you approach it with fresh eyes. Remember, this was part of your self-editing prep.

Once you return with fresh eyes, follow the thread of your story with a mix of curiosity and suspicion. Every major action, reveal, discovery, and character decision should hold up under basic scrutiny:

- Would this really happen?
- Would this character—this specific character—make that choice?
- Does this contradict something stated earlier?
- Is this set up properly?
- Did the story resolve what was promised?

Original:

> Saul Goodman is on the run and highly wanted after Heisenberg dies. He leaves Albuquerque and settles in Omaha as a Cinnabon manager, Gene. He encounters Marion and her son Jeff. On a phone call with Gene, Marion tells him about Jeff's criminal activities in Albuquerque and how she had to deal with bondsmen. "Gene" responds that bondsmen aren't needed in Omaha, as Omaha isn't like Albuquerque. Since Gene said he has never lived in Albuquerque, Marion is suspicious and types in "conman" and "Albuquerque" and finds out that Gene is Saul, which leads to his arrest.

Marion brings up Albuquerque's laws and the need for bondsmen. Gene simply responds that Omaha works differently—it's "not like Albuquerque at all." She fed him the information, so he wasn't revealing any intimate knowledge of a place he claimed never to have lived. He was just responding to what she gave him. And even if she suspected he'd lied about Albuquerque, why would that lead her to search "conman"? That's a very specific leap from one suspected lie. (This plot hole caused a fight between my hubby and me. But, he was right . . . shhh, don't tell him I said so.)

Revised:

> Marion just tells him about Jeff's problems with the law, but she doesn't mention bondsmen. Saul says, "Well, at least you don't have to deal with bondsmen like you would in Albuquerque," then quickly pivots and says, "I haven't lived in Albuquerque. It's just that a buddy of mine went through something similar there." He offers this explanation quickly before she even questions him. She gets off the phone and recalls how she met him when he was looking for his lost dog, Nippy, in front of her house, but then he seemed confused when she asked him about Nippy later. She searches for "Albuquerque criminal," and she sees Saul Goodman, who looks like Gene.

When you spot a plot hole, you have options for how to fix it. The fix can be simple:

- If events contradict each other, correct the details in one place so they align.
- If something is unexplained, add a sentence, hint, or earlier setup that makes the discovery feel earned rather than random.
- If a character makes an illogical choice, strengthen their motivation or rewrite the moment so their actions make sense for who they are.
- If something is impossible, determine whether it's truly necessary, if it is, give your world or your characters the tools or rules that make the impossible suddenly plausible.
- If you left a storyline unresolved, either bring it to a meaningful close or cut the setup entirely so you don't make a promise you can't keep.

Other times, the fix is bigger, and you need to

- go back and plant seeds in earlier chapters if you have a late-breaking reveal that wasn't set up early enough
- rewrite an implausible event, shifting entirely who takes action or how the moment unfolds
- add in a new scene or two to fix a storyline that had vanished and been forgotten about

Occasionally, you'll find a plot hole so foundational that the best solution is restructuring the surrounding scenes so events unfold in a more believable order.

As you revise, you'll need to read like someone who hasn't lived inside your book for months. Notice the rules you've set and the promises you've made—whether intentional or not—and make sure every scene honors them. You want to give your readers the gift of a fully intact plot. This separates a good story from one readers will rave about.

Self-editing in practice

Original A:

Marcus leaned against the balcony rail, tapping his pen against the open notebook. He stared at the half-filled page, frustrated. *If only the words would come.* With a sigh, he snapped the notebook shut, set it on the balcony, and went back inside.

Later, when his roommate knocked, Marcus called out, "Just a second!" He glanced at his desk and scribbled down a few more lines before opening the door (generated by ChatGPT).

> **PAUSE HERE**
>
> Open your personalized workbook on your computer and review the practice exercise, asking
>
> - Do any details contradict what the story has already established?
> - Does every action or development logically follow the previous one?
> - Does anything feel confusing, inconsistent, or missing?
>
> After answering, come up with a few ways to revise the issue before reading my revision.

Problem with original:

Earlier, Marcus had closed the notebook and left it on the balcony, but then he was seen writing in it at his desk with no mention of having retrieved it.

Revised A (two ideas):

- Cut out the last line of the first paragraph.
- Have Marcus close the notebook and bring it inside with him; then he can open it on his desk.

Original B:

Lena bit her lip as the crowd surged around the courthouse steps. The police presence was overwhelming—riot gear, shields, and barricades.

Lena slipped between two officers, ducked under the caution tape, and strolled right into the building. Moments later, she was sitting in the front row of the trial, unnoticed.

> ### PAUSE HERE
>
> - Do any details contradict what the story has already established?
>
> - Does every action or development logically follow the previous one?
>
> - Does anything feel confusing, inconsistent, or missing?
>
> After answering, come up with a solution before reading my revision.

Problem with original:

While not entirely impossible, it's highly unlikely Lena could have bypassed heavy police security.

Revised B (two ideas):

- Have Lena disguised as a police officer.
- Have a friend distract the police so she can slip through.

EDITING STEPS

❑ Ask questions to check for contradictions, unexplained events, illogical events, impossible events, and/or unresolved events within a scene and throughout the story thread:
- Does the story present two facts that can't both be true?
- Do any events occur without sufficient setup or explanation?
- Do any objects, places, or plot devices appear without any hint of origin or cause?
- Would a reader reasonably expect an explanation for an event that wasn't delivered?
- Do any major outcomes feel unearned or implausible based on what the story has established?
- Are there moments when the plot conveniently solves itself without enough groundwork?
- Do any plot points feel too easy, lucky, or forced?
- Do any events break the internal logic or rules of the story world?
- Did any subplots remain unresolved?
- At the end of the story, do any lingering questions remain that a reader would expect to have been addressed?

❑ Revise any issues spotted.

❑ Use beta readers to find plot holes that you were too close to the manuscript to see.

Organize the Timeline Effectively

Timeline issues are usually simple to correct, but they're surprisingly easy to miss. This is one of the areas I track closely when editing, because even small inconsistencies can pull readers out of the story.

The most straightforward way to address this issue is to actually create a timeline, listing how many days have passed (and the day of the week, if you know it) since the last scene. Doing so helps you spot timeline issues.

For example, in one novel I edited, the number of days that had passed between scenes indicated the current scene took place on a Saturday; however, the characters were talking about going to school the next day, which clearly wouldn't work. In another novel I edited, the character said it had been three months since the virus had started, but the first outbreak had occurred five months earlier. I never would have caught these issues without tracking the timeline.

I track timelines using a chart like this one, starting a new row for each new day.

Day/Date	Events	Chapter #
Day 1	Events that happen this day	1
	Events that happen this day Events that happen this day Events that happen this day Events that happen this day	2 3 4
Two days after chapter 4	Events Events	5 6
	Events Events	7
	Events Events	8
Saturday	Events Events Events	9
Next day (Sun)	Events	10

Notice how some dates are blank. You don't always need to explicitly state how many days have passed between every scene or what day of the week it is. It's fine to not always know this information. But when you do have context clues or give specific timestamps for given events, the timeline needs to match up. So track the known clues and make sure everything aligns.

Original:

Chapter 3: On a Wednesday morning, Priya notes in her journal: "Two weeks until the gallery show. I need to finish three more paintings."

Chapter 4: Priya is at the dinner party, and a friend asks how the paintings are coming. "I have eleven days," she tells him, stress creeping into her voice. But she mentions being grateful tomorrow is Sunday so she can have a day off and enjoy church.

Chapter 5: She comments it was such a good thing she enjoyed church yesterday because today was so busy. The gallery owner confirms with her that she'll be ready for the show a week from Friday.

Day/Date	Events	Chapter #
Wednesday (stated in the text)	Writes in her journal that the gallery is two weeks away and she's looking forward to the dinner party on Friday.	3
3 days later (Saturday . . . since she has church tomorrow)	At a dinner party. Says she has eleven days and looking forward to church tomorrow.	4
2 days later (Monday since yesterday was Sunday)	Busy day at work. Confirms show for a week from Friday	5

Journal said the party was on a Friday, but it has to be on a Saturday since church is the next day. Then, at the dinner party, in chapter 4, she says she has eleven days, but on Monday, the show is a week from that Friday, which is thirteen days from chapter 4. I don't see an issue with writing that the gallery is two weeks away in chapter 3 when it's really two weeks and two days because we approximate like that.

Revised:

> The easiest fix would be to have her write in her journal that the dinner party is on Saturday and then mention it's thirteen days away when she's at the dinner party.

Self-editing in practice

Original:

> The train finally pulled into Brighton just before dusk, its wheels squealing as it slowed. Caleb stretched his legs, stiff from the eight-hour ride. He checked into a small inn near the harbor, dropped his bag on the bed, and went out to find dinner. The seafood place down the street smelled promising, and he lingered there until late, savoring fried cod and listening to the gulls outside.
>
> The next morning, sunlight streamed across the room. He spent the day wandering the pier, sketching boats in his notebook, and buying trinkets from the market stalls. That night, he wrote in his journal about how different the sea air felt compared to the city.
>
> On his third day in Brighton, Caleb woke to the sound of church bells. He decided to take a ferry tour along the coast, snapping photos until the memory card was full. By evening, he was sunburned and exhausted.
>
> Two days later, he mailed a postcard home, writing: *"I have been here a full week now, and it's been everything I hoped for"* (generated by ChatGPT).

PAUSE HERE

Open your personalized workbook on your computer and review the practice exercise, asking

- Does the sequence of events unfold in a clear, trackable order?

- Can you tell how much time passes between events?

- Does any moment feel rushed or out of order?

After answering, provide a revised fix before reading my revision.

Problem with original:

Caleb said he's been there a week, but if you track it all, he's only been there for five days.

Tracked timeline:

Day/Date	Events	Chapter #
Day 1	Arrived and got dinner	1
Day 2	Wandered the pier and sketched	1
Day 3	Took a ferry tour	1
Day 5	Mailed postcard and said it had been a week	1

Revised (two ideas):

- Can change the postcard to say "I have been here nearly a week."
- Could add more days spent there before he sends the postcard.

EDITING STEPS

❑ Track your timeline. (You can do this however you want.)

❑ Highlight any discrepancies in the timeline. (I do this by highlighting problematic days or events in the tracked chart.)

❑ Make changes to ensure the timeline matches up.

Characters

Throughout the character topics, I often refer to a singular character, but if you have multiple main characters, then follow the advice for each one.

Make Them Believable

Many readers turn to stories to escape, but that escape only works if the characters feel real. Readers need to see someone they recognize—some version of themselves, a friend, a sibling, an ex, a coworker—reflected on the page. When a character isn't believable, the spell breaks, and it becomes much harder for readers to care, connect, or keep turning pages.

During the initial drafting process, writers build characters in different ways. Some start with a detailed character sketch for each main character and essential side characters before they even write the plot. Others prefer to discover their characters slowly as they write, letting motivations, tics, and flaws emerge on the page. Neither approach is superior. The goal in both is to create strong, believable characters.

To ensure your characters are believable, check that each has a unique personality with a mix of strengths and weaknesses, consistent behavior, and emotional logic, and that they're grounded in the scene.

Caveat

You may only need to work on one or two of the subtopics within this topic, so feel free to skip to the sections you need.

Believable, unique personality

All people have a mix of strengths and weaknesses. No one is entirely evil or good (though some come pretty close to one or the other end of the spectrum). If any of your main characters or essential side characters are one-dimensional (all good or all bad), then start there. Make sure to give your protagonist and other "good" characters some flaws and ensure your villainous characters have some redeeming qualities. That's the basis of a good character.

From there, if your main characters feel flat or aimless, you may need to pause and build or refine a character sketch. A sketch at this stage can help you articulate each character's backstory, experiences, and formative pressures (genetic and environmental) that have shaped who they are, making it easier to revise scenes that reflect their unique personality. At the very least, you need to know your character's goal, feelings about their goal, how those emotions change throughout the story, and what's at stake for them.

Use the prompts below for each character who needs a clearer personality. From here on out, I refer to a single character, but if you have multiple characters who feel flat or aimless, you may need to create a character sketch for each.

How to use these prompts

- Choose selectively. You don't need to answer all of these. This isn't an interrogation. Think of these prompts as menu options. Grab the ones that help you understand your character and ignore the rest.

- Go as deep as you need. If your character isn't fully fleshed out and readers—or worse, you—can't adequately describe them, you may need a more extensive sketch. You may only need to answer a few questions.

- Add context. If a question asks for a quick answer ("introvert or extrovert?"), answer and explain why.

BACKSTORY

- How many siblings do they have, and where do they fall in the birth order?
- What was their economic status growing up?
- How did their parents treat them?
- What was their relationship like with their parents and siblings?
- What was their greatest achievement to date?
- What were they like as a child (whatever would be younger than their age at the start of the book)?
- What's the most traumatic thing to have happened to them? (Everyone has trauma, whether mild or big.)
- What was their first kiss like?
- What's the worst thing they did to someone they loved?
- What's the worst thing they have ever done?
- What do they regret?
- What were their childhood ambitions?
- What's their best and worst memory?
- How popular were they in school?
- What grades did they get in school?
- What were their favorite subjects?
- Who were their favorite teachers?
- What activities were they involved with in school?
- What was their biggest struggle as a child, as a teenager, as a young adult?
- What past jobs have they had? How did they feel about those jobs?
- Have they ever been bullied or teased?
- What religion were they raised in, if any?
- How did/do they view their religion?
- Do they have any disabilities?
- Are they in good health?

> **Caveat**
>
> While creating a backstory can help you form a more believable and unique character, this doesn't mean all the backstory details should appear on the page (see the avoid Info dumping topic on page 175). You should only reveal what the reader needs to know, when they need to know it. You're mostly using this sketch to understand how your character will act, react, speak, and make decisions in your actual scenes.

PERSONALITY INFORMED BY BACKSTORY

Once you understand the experiences that shaped your character, look at how those experiences show up in their personality. Again, choose only the questions that clarify who they are on the page.

- What type of clothes do they wear?
- What words or phrases do they use a lot?
- Are they optimistic or pessimistic?
- Are they introverted or extroverted? (What traits of introversion or extroversion do they have?)
- What bad habits do they have?
- How do they display affection?
- How do they want to be seen by others?
- How do they see themselves?
- How competitive are they?
- What would be their result on various personality tests? (Enneagram, Disc, Myers-Briggs, color code, etc.)
- What are their strongest and best traits?
- What are their weakest traits?
- How do they react to praise, criticism, differences of opinion?
- What do they fear?
- What are their secrets?

- What are their wounds?
- What's their philosophy of life?
- What makes them cry?
- What are their political views?
- How do they treat people they like? How do they treat people they don't like?
- What do they value most in a friend?
- What's their most treasured possession?
- What are their pet peeves?
- How do they respond to a threat?
- How do they perceive strangers?
- How do they handle conflict with others?
- Are they more of a leader or a follower?
- What are their talents?
- What religious beliefs do they currently hold?
- What are their top values?
- What gets them out of bed?
- What's their moral code?
- What are their routines and habits?
- How do they keep their home?
- What's their favorite thing to do with friends? By themselves?
- What are their favorites? (Animal, food, color, place to visit, song, book, movie, etc.)
- What's their idea of perfect happiness?

Consistent personality

Perhaps your characters already have unique personalities with strengths and weaknesses, but they don't always remain true to their personality.

This doesn't mean a character can't change their attitude or preferences or do something unpredictable or contradictory. People sometimes act out of character and can evolve.

But when this happens, it must be clear in the text what caused the change.

Examples:

> If you have a character who constantly avoids confrontation and then suddenly throws punches in a bar fight without any cause, readers aren't going to buy it. You need a catalyst in there, like something pushed them past their breaking point (a threat to someone they love, a final humiliation that snaps something in them, liquid courage, etc.).

> If a doctor is a workaholic and centers their whole identity around work but then up and quits without a reason, this is inconsistent. Perhaps years of suppressed burnout finally erupted, or a patient's death shattered their world and brought on trauma every time they went to work.

When a character acts out of their established personality, it undermines believability. Instead, either have the character remain true to their personality, add an explanation for why they didn't, drop that plot point, or have the plot point come about in a different way. It doesn't work to have a character do something just because you need them to. The character's choices should drive the plot, not the other way around.

Emotional logic

I can't tell you how many reviews say a character felt "too stupid to be believable." When a character consistently ignores obvious clues, refuses to connect dots any reasonable person would connect, or makes choices that defy basic logic, readers stop trusting them.

This isn't to say a character can never have a moment of poor judgment. Humans absolutely have moments when emotion clouds logic. We panic, deny, avoid, lash out, you name it. Characters should have those moments too. Emotional logic doesn't mean characters must be rational all the time; it means their emotional reactions must make sense given who they are and what they have lived through.

HOW TO MAINTAIN EMOTIONAL LOGIC

- Reach plausible conclusions based on the information your character has. Even if their conclusion is wrong, it should still be a conclusion a reasonable person in their emotional state might reach.
- Have emotional responses tied to their backstory or internal wounds. If fear, grief, or shame clouds their judgment, show why.
- Course-correct once the emotions settle. Denial can't last forever. Eventually, your character needs to reassess.
- Avoid plot-required stupidity. If the only reason the character makes a bad choice is to move the plot forward, readers will feel it immediately.

Make sure your characters, especially your protagonists, come to logical conclusions more often than not. You want your readers to trust them.

Example (Amara is guarded and slow to trust):

> Amara set her coffee down and slid into the booth across from the woman she'd met twenty minutes ago in the waiting room.
>
> "So what do you do?" the woman asked.
>
> "Graphic designer. Freelance, mostly." Amara wrapped both hands around her mug. "It's fine. Not what I planned, honestly. I wanted to be an illustrator—children's books, that kind of thing—but my mom always said art wasn't a real career, so I sort of just . . . stopped trying." She laughed quietly. "Twelve years later and I'm still a little bitter about it, I think."
>
> The woman smiled. "Moms, right?"
>
> "Yeah." Amara glanced out the window. "She passed last year, so I don't know. It's complicated" (generated by Claude).

Amara tells a stranger way too much information for a guarded charac-ter. The writer has essentially made her confide in a stranger because the plot needed that backstory delivered. This backstory should be revealed in another way rather than having the character act illogically.

Grounded in the scene

Characters don't exist in a vacuum; they react to their surroundings and the people around them. They shouldn't enter every scene and immedi-ately start talking. In some scenes, sure. But in others, they need to take in what's around them and respond before diving into dialogue.

Think about it. When you watch a movie, an actor doesn't just act when they're delivering their lines. They're acting throughout the scene because they're reacting to the

- words the other character is saying
- physical setting
- emotions of the other characters
- events unfolding around them

Of course, you don't want to overdo it and show your character reacting to everything. This would make for a very long novel—and a boring one at that. Characters won't respond to every word, setting detail emotional shift, or event. But if your character never or rarely responds to what's happening around them, then you have a believability problem.

You can pick key moments to show your character's reactions in several ways. The most obvious is to show how they feel. Feelings help readers get to know a character:

- If they feel scared when they get into a car, that says something about them.
- If they feel confident stepping onto a stage in front of a large audience, that says something about them.
- If they react negatively to their mom saying, "I love you," that says something about them.

But reactions can also be physical, sensory, or behavioral. What do they notice about their surroundings? What do they hear, smell, taste, touch, and see? Don't forget to use all your character's senses.

You also need to think of your character as you create their reactions. No two people will describe an environment or situation the same way. Show how your character views things in that moment. (Notice I said "in that moment" because how one views their environment can change based on their current state of mind.)

Original:

Erika walked into the abandoned warehouse. "I got your message," she said to Kevin. "What's so urgent that you needed to meet here?"

Kevin crossed his arms. "We need to talk about the money you owe me. I have been patient, but my patience is running out."

"I told you I'd get it to you by the end of the month. Why are you being so dramatic about this?"

Kevin stepped closer. "Dramatic? You have been saying that for three months now. I want my money, Erika, or there will be consequences."

"Fine, I'll have it to you next week. Can I go now? I have dinner plans."

Erika enters a creepy, isolated location to meet someone she owes money to—someone who's now threatening her—yet she shows zero awareness of the danger. A real person would be hyper-aware of every shadow and sound. Instead, Erika acts like they're having coffee at Starbucks, making her feel less like a living, breathing character and more like a talking head delivering plot information.

Revised:

Erika stepped through the warehouse's rusted side door, and the temperature dropped ten degrees. The vast space swallowed sound, leaving only the distant drip of water somewhere in the darkness and her footsteps echoing off concrete.

"I got your message," Erika said, staying near the door. "What's so urgent that you needed to meet here?"

"We need to talk about the money you owe me. I have been patient, but my patience is running out."

Erika tightened her grip on her phone in her pocket. "I told you I'd get it to you by the end of the month. Why are you being so dramatic about this?"

"Dramatic?" Kevin took two steps forward. The fluorescent light overhead flickered. "You have been saying that for three months now. I want my money, Erika, or there will be consequences."

She forced herself to hold his gaze, though her throat felt dry. "Fine. Next week. But I need to go. I have dinner plans."

I added in setting details in her voice, showing her mood and feelings. Then I also added in some action beats to make her a believable character reacting to the environment.

Self-editing in practice

Original (This is the opening chapter):

Jennifer walked into her childhood home for the first time in ten years. "Hi, Mom," she said.

Her mother stood up from the couch. "Jennifer! I'm so glad you came back. I have missed you so much."

"Yeah, me too." Jennifer sat down. "So, Dad's funeral is tomorrow?"

"Yes, at ten o'clock. The whole family will be there."

Jennifer nodded. "Okay, sounds good. I'll be there." She pulled out her phone and checked her messages. "Do you mind if I invite some friends over later? I thought we could have a barbecue."

Her mother smiled. "Of course, honey. Whatever you want."

"Great. Oh, and I was thinking—since I'm here anyway, maybe I'll stay for a few months. I could finally finish that novel I have been working on. This house is so peaceful."

"That would be wonderful! Your old room is exactly how you left it."

Jennifer stood up. "Perfect. I'm going to grab some coffee. Want anything?" She headed toward the kitchen, humming a tune (generated by Claude).

PAUSE HERE

Open your personalized workbook on your computer and review the practice exercise, asking

- Does the character's behavior feel natural and consistent with their motivations?
- Does the character react to their environment?
- Does the reader need to know any background or context here?

After answering, revise the passage before reading my explanation of the issue and my revision.

Problems with original:

Jennifer's emotional response isn't consistent with someone who hasn't been home in ten years and whose father just died. The reader would need some backstory to understand why she hasn't been home in ten years, why she doesn't react to the physical environment, and why she doesn't display a clear personality; otherwise, she doesn't feel like a real person.

Revised:

Jennifer went to knock, then hesitated, resting her hand on the doorknob of her childhood home. Ten years. The paint was still that same faded yellow her father had refused to change, and the porch still creaked under her weight in precisely the spot she remembered.

She pushed the door open. The smell hit her first: her mother's lavender sachets mixed with something else, something stale and medicinal that hadn't been there before.

"Jennifer?" Her mother appeared from the living room, thinner than Jennifer remembered, with new lines around her eyes.

"Hi, Mom."

Her mother's face crumpled, and she crossed the room quickly, pulling Jennifer into a hug. Jennifer froze, then forced herself to return a quick hug before pulling away.

"I'm so glad you came back," her mother whispered. "I wasn't sure you would."

"Of course I came." Even as she said it, she could hear the lie. Missing three Christmases, not returning phone calls, leaving a decade ago after the big fight all spoke louder than her words.

She looked past her mother to the living room. Dad's recliner sat empty, his reading glasses still folded on the side table. Her throat tightened.

"The funeral's tomorrow," her mother said. "Ten o'clock."

She nodded, not trusting her voice. She should say something comforting, something a good daughter would say. But the words wouldn't come. She'd imagined this moment a hundred times—coming home, making peace with her father—and now it was too late.

"I kept your room the same," her mother continued, filling the silence. "In case you ever . . . well. It's there if you want it."

"Thanks." She picked up her bag. "I think I need to lie down for a bit."

She climbed the stairs, each step familiar under her feet, and stopped at her bedroom door. Band posters still on the walls. The same blue bedspread. It was like walking into a time capsule of the person she used to be, the person who'd slammed this door and screamed that she hated it here.

While we don't yet know the fight that caused Jennifer to leave, I added in the fact that she left because of a fight (backstory) and hated it here. Other details of her backstory can be revealed later, but I gave just enough here to help the character make sense. She now has a clear personality—she struggles with emotional expression (quick hug and doesn't say "I love you" or "miss you"). I also added in character-specific observations (her dad's glasses, the swing), revealing information about her personality and relationship with other characters. Her emotional reactions are now complex like a real person (guilt, grief, discomfort), she now reacts to her environment, and she overall feels more believable.

EDITING STEPS

❑ Ensure each major character has a believable, unique personality:
- Does the character have both strengths and weaknesses?
- Can you explain how their past shaped their personality?
- Can you identify defining traits that separate them from other characters?

❑ Anytime a character "acts out of character," either ensure a clear catalyst exists or change that moment for them to act true to character, even if that changes the plot point.

❑ For each major decision, reaction, or moment of judgment, ensure logical thinking for their current emotional state:
- Does their conclusion make sense based on the information they have?
- Is their emotional response tied to their backstory, wounds, or personality?
- Do they eventually reassess once their emotional spike settles?

❑ For each scene, add selective reactions if the character isn't grounded:
- Does the character respond to what's happening around them?
- Do they occasionally notice or interpret something based on their mood, fear, stress, or internal conflict?
- Are they a participant in the scene rather than a talking head?

Ensure They're Dynamic

Think about the last book you couldn't put down. Was the main character waiting for things to happen, or were they out there making terrible, desperate choices that kept you turning pages at 2 a.m.?

Dynamic characters keep readers turning pages. All your main characters should be dynamic in two essential ways: They have agency, and they undergo growth. These two elements work together to create compelling, memorable characters that readers care about and believe in.

Give them clear goals

The character may not be consciously aware of their goals, but they still have them. So make sure both you and the reader are clear about what the character wants. Otherwise, they're wandering without a clear direction, and it's harder for your readers to feel invested. Ask, What does my character want above all else, and why? Of course, we have lots of wants and desires, but these wants typically add up to one bigger thing. Try to get to that big thing.

Example:

> I may want to:
>
> - Communicate better with my kids
> - Market my products better and get more sales

- Think more positively

But ultimately, what all these add up to is the desire to be and feel successful. That's the overall goal.

Once you have the ultimate story goal, ask, What does my character want in this scene? They should have a clear motivation and goal for each scene. These are the little wants and desires that lead to the bigger motivation. (Yes, that means your character's scene-level goals will change throughout the story.)

Note that this doesn't mean explicitly spelling those goals out. To make it clear to the reader, you can reveal each character's goals through internal thoughts, actions, and dialogue. Readers can read between the lines.

Give them agency

Now that your character has goals, they need agency, which means they drive the story forward. They can't be a passive observer as the plot unfolds around them; otherwise, no matter how exciting those events are, the story will feel flat. They have to continually take action. They'll sometimes take the wrong action; I mean, everyone is flawed. But the important part is that they're *taking action.*

To ensure their actions come across as authentic, use the character's goals to inform the realistic choices they would make in any given situation, and then have them act on those choices. Notice I said "realistic" choices, not perfect choices. We don't always make perfect decisions, but we make choices that are true to ourselves in that moment—shaped by our objectives, thoughts, worldview, feelings, and circumstances. A character who consistently makes convenient choices solely because the plot requires it will ring false to readers. When readers know your character well, they can sense when a decision clashes with that character's internal logic or lacks a clear reason for an out-of-character choice. But if they can't feel that difference, it's a sign the character's personality hasn't been established clearly enough. In other words, you have a believability, unique personality problem (see the previous topic).

Example:

> Imagine this series of plot events: Nikki got a call from her boss, telling her she'd been promoted. The next day, her neighbor knocked on her door and invited her to a party where she happened to meet James, who asked for her number. A week later, James called and asked her on a date. At the restaurant, James suggested they order the special, and Nikki agreed. After dinner, James proposed they take a walk in the park. When they reached the fountain, James told Nikki he thought they should be exclusive.

> *The plot happens to her rather than because of her. She doesn't make any meaningful choices based on her desires and doesn't take any risks. This results in a flat, forgettable character who feels more like a prop than a person.*

Original:

> Consider a story about a farm boy who dreams of adventure. His aunt and uncle are killed by soldiers, forcing him to leave home. An old man tells him to come along on a mission, so he does. They need a pilot, so they hire one at a bar. The pilot's ship gets pulled into a space station by a tractor beam. While trapped there, he sees a princess who needs rescuing, so he goes to save her. The old man dies fighting a villain. Later, commanders tell him to join an attack on the space station, and he succeeds in destroying it.

> *The farm boy is just being swept along by circumstances and other people's decisions.*

Revised:

> Luke finds his aunt and uncle murdered. Despite his fear, he chooses to leave with Obi-Wan rather than stay and bury them because he wants revenge and purpose. When Obi-Wan explains they need transport, Luke suggests Mos Eisley even though it's dangerous. After Han is hired, Luke argues to rescue Leia against Han's protests. Luke sees an opportunity and seizes it, even hatching the prisoner transfer ruse himself. When Obi-Wan sacrifices himself, Luke has to decide whether to flee or honor that sacrifice by staying in the fight. At the Death Star trench, he makes the critical choice to trust the Force over his targeting computer, rejecting the "safe" option for what he believes is right.

Now Luke is making active choices that shape the story, even when reacting to circumstances beyond his control.

PASSIVITY AS A CHARACTER TRAIT

Some people are passive by nature, and so are some characters. But passivity as a character trait is different than passivity in the plot. If the character chooses to be passive and that choice influences what happens next, then they aren't lacking agency. For example, a character who avoids confrontation and doesn't speak up for themselves is passive as a character trait. They're not necessarily *being* passive in the plot. Not speaking up for themselves can affect what happens next, so they're still considered active, as their agency created change.

Give them growth

Before you start revising for growth, identify how your character started and how they ended. Was there a change? Your main characters should grow by the end of the story. However, growth doesn't always mean positive change. Growth is any meaningful transformation, whether positive or negative.

- Insecure → Confident: A character learns to trust their abilities and speak up for themselves.
- Kind → Jaded: A character's compassion erodes after repeated betrayals, leaving them cynical and harsh.
- Naive → Wise: Experience teaches hard lessons that shift a character's understanding of the world.
- Hopeful → Defeated: Circumstances break a character's spirit and optimism.[1]

This transformation is tied to your underlying theme (the big idea your story is exploring), as your character arc shows that theme becoming visible on the page, whether your character rises or falls. In a positive arc, the character moves toward a healthier or more constructive understanding of the theme. In a negative arc, the character embraces a damaging belief or doubles down on a destructive worldview, which still expresses the theme but as tragedy or caution. Growth doesn't always mean "becoming better." Just make sure to show how the character's internal evolution (or devolution) reveals the theme.

Original:

Imagine a story about Gary, a successful lawyer who takes on a high-profile case defending someone he believes is innocent. Over the course of the story, he

- discovers evidence that challenges his initial belief
- faces pressure from his firm to drop the case
- has a strained marriage due to the long hours
- learns the justice system has flaws he never noticed before

---

1   AI drafted the list, and I strengthened and edited the output.

- wins the case but realizes the defendant was guilty after all

At the end, Gary returns to his office, takes on another case, and approaches it exactly as he did before: with the same assumptions and confidence. Essentially, the events changed nothing about how he sees himself, his work, or the world.

This is a character who experienced a plot but underwent no character arc. The story feels hollow because Gary ends exactly where he began.

Revised:

> With the next case, he requests a meeting with his firm's partners and proposes a new internal review process for how they vet cases. They push back. He pushes harder, which costs him a friendship and puts him on shaky ground with the partners. Now he has to decide what kind of lawyer and man he wants to be.

Remember, character growth is tied to theme. In the case of Gary, his change and decision bring the justice theme to the forefront.

Self-editing in practice

Original (character arc from a novel I edited):

> A drone from the oppressive government scours her city. She tells the city it's bad news, and they prepare. A bunch of castoffs fight and kill everyone in her city while she hides.
>
> She flees into the wilderness with a vague intention of going north to meet with the rebellion. She stays with a tribe, learns their ways, and only leaves when she's accused of something and will be killed if she stays.

She accidentally stumbles upon a forgotten university and stays there for years, learning. One day she decides to recruit other students. She finds two students and teaches them, then decides to recruit more years later. One of her students makes a mistake, and the enemy forces them to evacuate, which only works because her mentor sacrifices himself.

While fleeing, she encounters the guy who wiped out her village. She lives because he assumes she'll die of thirst. One day she remembers her grandma had told her to go north, so she goes back to that original plan.

Once in the north, she leads the charge with all her knowledge and insists on fighting with expertise rather than violence but gets betrayed. She thwarts the rebellion's violent plans but ends up accidentally causing violence herself.

Because of the betrayal, she and her students leave the rebellion in the north.

PAUSE HERE

Open your personalized workbook on your computer and review the practice exercise, asking

- Can you identify what the character wants throughout the story?

- Do you see ways the character changes (or fails to change)?

- Do the character's choices affect the plot, or do things just happen to them?

After answering, revise the character arc before reading my revision.

Problems with original:

She is passive for too long. Her motivations don't drive her; she drifts into whatever comes her way (a tribe, a university) rather than following a clear motivation (going north to the rebellion). She takes significant detours, seemingly dropping her goal. She spends years just learning and being taught before she takes any action and decides to recruit students.

Revised character arc:

- She rescues a few people from her village during the initial attack, but they're too scared to go north with her.
- She seeks out the tribe, hoping to form an alliance. When she's accused, she fights to prove her innocence, but time is running out, so she chooses to leave and find a different alliance.
- Following her grandmother's cryptic stories, she searches for the rumored university. When she finds it, she convinces the guy living there to mentor her, telling him she believes knowledge is the weapon she needs to take to the rebellion in the north.
- After learning for a brief time, she builds a movement with a clear goal: rebuild knowledge to bring recruits to the rebellion who can fight with more than just violence.
- She orchestrates a clear extraction plan, but something goes wrong, and her mentor has to sacrifice himself.
- When she meets the castoff in the wilderness, she opts not to kill him to avoid vengeance and the cycle of violence.
- The rest continues the same, as she's active at the end.

In this new arc, you can see how her choices drive her forward.

EDITING STEPS

❏ Check each scene to ensure the main character has a clear, small goal that leads to the overall goal. If they don't, revise to give the protagonist a goal in that scene and add stakes if they don't meet it (the motivation they need).

❏ Check that the character creates meaningful change in each scene through their choices, driven by their desire to achieve their goal. If they don't, increase the pressure on them and create a clear choice.

❏ Verify that your character makes a deliberate choice at the inciting incident or turning points and then continues to choose that path (or double down on it) as conflicts test them.

❏ Ensure your character makes both good and bad choices, maybe even making them culpable for the fallout.

❏ If your character is lacking overall change, diagnose the gap by asking:
  - What theme are you exploring in the novel?
  - How is the character initially misaligned with that theme?
  - What events will force them to shift toward (or away from) this theme by the end?
  - How does the external plot pressure or mirror this internal shift?

❏ Map your character's arc: Identify who they are at the beginning and who they are at the end. Identify two or three key moments when they should show signs of this transformation and add those in.

Create Good Secondary Characters

Many of us have watched a spinoff show that features a side character from the original story. I'm currently watching *Better Call Saul* after having watched *Breaking Bad*. Saul was a side character in *Breaking Bad*, and fans loved him so much, he got his own show. In *Breaking Bad*, though, he was very much a *side* character. He didn't steal the focus from Walter White and the other main characters.

And that's the key. Side characters should serve a purpose, be unique, and not overshadow the main character (MC). Do note that I use MC throughout, but you could have more than one MC.

Give them a purpose in the story

Side characters shouldn't just take up space. Every side character should serve a role.

- Plot function: providing information, creating obstacles, offering resources
- Character function: helping or hindering your MC (foil, mentor, comic relief, voice of reason, or another antagonist)
- Thematic function: challenging the protagonist, embodying opposing values, helping the MC learn the theme[2]

---

2   AI assisted in brainstorming this list to ensure completeness.

If they don't serve a purpose, ask, Would the story change if I removed this character? If it wouldn't, cut the character or revise them so they serve a purpose. If your side characters all serve the same or similar purposes, consider combining them.

Examples of a necessary character (ChatGPT gave me these examples):

Mercutio in *Romeo and Juliet* escalates the feud, pushing Romeo to seek revenge. His purpose is to advance the plot.

Draco Malfoy in the *Harry Potter* series challenges Harry Potter's worldview. His prejudice forces Harry to define himself against those values.

Samwise Gamgee in *The Lord of the Rings* series reveals the themes of friendship, perseverance, and the power of ordinary people.

Example of an unnecessary character:

Melinda is a rookie detective investigating a string of art thefts. She has a mentor guiding her, a rival detective competing with her, and a key suspect who keeps throwing her off track.

Enter Roberto.

Roberto is Melinda's neighbor. He works at a grocery store and loves collecting rare stamps. He occasionally shows up to chat about the weather, complain about his cat, or mention his stamp collection.

But the mystery unfolds the same without him; he doesn't challenge Melinda by offering insight or conflict, reveal a theme, or deepen her character. Their conversations are shallow and reveal nothing about her.

Unless Roberto suddenly becomes the mastermind behind the thefts or provides a crucial clue, he's just filler. Even if he does offer a clue, like stating that the stolen painting looks like one of his rare stamps, if he seems useless the rest of the time, you can cut out his other scenes entirely. Alternatively, you might be better served by merging his role with that of a more relevant character. Maybe the rival detective has a stamp hobby, so he gives the clue.

Make them their own person

You don't need to create entire backstories for your side characters, but you may need some backstory details to shape them. For example, you don't need to know a bartender's whole childhood, but knowing he started tending bar after his restaurant failed explains why he's defensive about criticism of his cooking. Perhaps that backstory appears on page; perhaps it doesn't. Either way, it shapes how he acts on the page.

So determine a few details about your side characters that make them who they are. While they won't need to be as developed as your MC, your side characters still need to be real and unique.

DEVELOP DISTINCTIVE TRAITS

Use meaningful details to give side characters a personality. These could be quirks, speech patterns, or a defining habit. Keep these details focused on what makes the character distinct without diverting attention from the protagonist.

Examples of small details:

- A bartender who constantly misquotes famous sayings
- A neighbor who follows a rigid schedule for when they get the mail, water their lawn, etc.
- A coworker who's always gossiping about others

These small touches make side characters feel real. As you add those touches, don't turn them into a caricature unless you're writing a melodrama, a K-drama, or using a caricature for satire (hello, *Mean Girls*), or some other such genre. The bulleted examples above could easily turn into caricatures if that was the only detail about them and it was exaggerated on the page. So notice I said use meaningful details (plural). So maybe that gossiping coworker is also the hardest worker.

GIVE THEM THEIR OWN LIVES

On top of having their own personality, side characters should have their own goals, conflicts, and unseen lives. For example, you can have a best friend who hints at their own work drama (but don't go on a side quest to show us details of said drama). That way, this character has a life separate from the MC.

But just like with backstory and personality traits, we don't need a full-blown character study here. Only reveal what's essential to your side character's purpose and what's critical to making them a real person: at least one non-caricature defining characteristic and some hints at goals and/or a life of their own.

Don't let them overshadow

Your side characters can be fun and engaging. They can be a joy to read about while your MC is annoying. That's fine. Your MC doesn't have to be more likable than the side characters, but they can't be overshadowed by them.

This means that while your side characters can have impactful moments and can even dominate scenes alongside the MC, the scene needs to ultimately serve the MC's story. For example, a side character gains the courage to stand up to a corrupt boss, inspiring the MC to stand up to her bully. In this scenario the side character's emotional arc rippled into the MC's arc rather than pulling readers away from it. When a side character's story can stand entirely on its own without affecting the MC, it's too large or too separate. Your side character shouldn't have more growth than the MC.

Original:

> Let's say a side character is estranged from their sister, and over the course of forty pages, they track their sister down, confront their shared grief over losing their mother, and reconcile. This steals too much focus, potentially leading readers to care more about this character's journey than the MC's.

The side character's arc is too dominant.

Revised:

> Perhaps she mentions being estranged from her sister at one point, gets a text from her and freezes, and later mentions they're talking again. Seeing the reconciliation could then give the MC the courage they need to accomplish their story goal.

Even if they don't steal the show with a separate arc, side characters can still detract if they have a more distinctive voice, deeper conflicts, and funnier and more exciting scenes. Again, it's okay if they're more likable. It's okay to give them funny lines (like Miracle Max in *The Princess Bride*). But if readers only enjoy scenes that include the side character, that's a problem.

Original:

> In a three-hundred-page novel about Olivia, a quiet, anxious college student navigating her first semester, her roommate, Jade, appears in only about fifty pages. But every single scene with Jade is electric:

- She has a razor-sharp wit and delivers amazing one-liners.
- She's fearless, confronting their RA, sneaking into campus events, saying exactly what she thinks.
- She has a mysterious past (dropped hints about why she left her last school).
- Her dialogue crackles, while Olivia's feels bland by comparison.
- She does most of the talking in their shared scenes.

Jade's small acts (like telling off a rude professor) feel more exciting than Olivia's entire arc of slowly making friends (generated by Claude).

Jade only shows up occasionally, but readers remember her scenes vividly, while Olivia's journey feels forgettable. Jade doesn't have that much page time, but she has all the personality, the best lines, the most interesting conflicts, and the more distinctive voice.

Revised idea:

Jade can still be witty and bold. In fact, that makes her an excellent foil to anxious Olivia. Keep her fearless personality and a few sharp one-liners, but remove the mysterious past that makes readers curious about her story instead of Olivia's.

Ensure that Olivia's goals, stakes, and outcomes are the primary focus in each scene.

Give her moments of unexpected courage that surprise even her. Maybe she's the one who tells off the rude professor, not in the same way Jade would do it, but in her own humble way.

Self-editing in practice

Original A:

For the sake of keeping the examples short, I put the end of the scene in a brief narrative summary rather than fleshing it all out.

> Riley knocked on the apartment door, juggling a grocery bag and a bottle of cheap wine. "Delivery for the world's most exhausted author!" she called.
>
> Katarina opened the door. "You didn't have to—"
>
> "Of course I did." Riley bustled inside, dropping the groceries on the counter. "You have been living on cereal and stress for three weeks. I'm staging an intervention." She unpacked pasta, sauce, garlic bread, and a chocolate bar the size of a textbook. "We feast, we brainstorm, and we celebrate your creative genius."
>
> "I wouldn't call it genius. I cut an entire chapter today."
>
> "Good!" Riley said, pointing a wooden spoon like a sword. "Slash and burn, baby. Out with the fluff, in with the glory!"
>
> By the time Riley finished cooking, she'd told three hilarious stories about her disastrous dating life, complete with impressions. Katarina mostly listened, and smiled for the first time all day (generated by ChatGPT).

> ## PAUSE HERE
>
> Open your personalized workbook on your computer and review the practice exercise, asking
>
> - Does this side character serve a clear purpose in the story?
>
> - Are they overshadowing the protagonist? If so, in what way?
>
> After answering, revise the scene to fix the issues you identified before reading my revision.

Problem with original:

It's fine that Riley has more humor and energy, while Katarina is less energetic. That's their mood in this given moment. It also works for Riley to do most of the talking. The problem is that we get no emotional arc from Katarina at all.

Revised:

> Riley knocked on the apartment door, juggling a grocery bag and a bottle of cheap wine. "Delivery for the world's most exhausted author!" she called.
>
> Katarina opened the door, manuscript still clutched in one hand. "You didn't have to—"
>
> "Of course I did." Riley bustled inside, dropping the groceries on the counter. "You have been living on cereal and stress for three weeks. I'm staging an intervention."
>
> She didn't need an intervention and could survive just fine on cereal, thank you very much. But the knot in her chest loosened up as Riley unpacked pasta, sauce, garlic bread, and a chocolate bar the size of a textbook. "I cut an entire chapter today."

"Good!" Riley said, pointing a wooden spoon like a sword. "Slash and burn, baby. Out with the fluff, in with the glory!"

"It was twenty pages." Katarina set the manuscript down, harder than she meant to. "Twenty pages I'll never get back."

Riley paused mid-stir. "But the book's better without it?"

She hesitated, then nodded. "Yeah. It is."

"Then those pages did their job." Riley grinned. "That's progress. That's a good thing. You know? Making the hard decisions. So let's feast and celebrate your creative genius."

By the time Riley finished cooking, she'd told three hilarious stories about her disastrous dating life, complete with impressions. Katarina laughed—actually laughed. Wow, she'd forgotten what that felt like.

She picked up her fork. Maybe Riley was right. Maybe cutting those pages meant she was finally getting somewhere.

Added thoughts and emotions to center Katarina. Riley still has the jokes and the upbeat personality, but now Katarina has some emotions as well and isn't overshadowed.

Original B:

Covey adjusted her headset and stared at the blinking cursor on her computer screen. She was supposed to submit her final project proposal by noon, but her brain felt like oatmeal.

"Still stuck?" her coworker, Jake, asked from the next cubicle. He leaned over the divider, holding his ever-present travel mug.

"Yeah," Covey said. "Can't get this section right."

Jake grinned. "You need caffeine. Want me to grab you a latte?"

She smiled. "Sure, thanks."

He disappeared. Ten minutes later, he was back, balancing two cups. They chatted about the new coffee shop downtown, about the weather, about nothing in particular.

By the time Jake left, the cursor still blinked accusingly. Covey sighed, took a sip, and went back to staring at the screen (generated by ChatGPT).

PAUSE HERE

- Does this side character serve a clear purpose in the story?
- Are they overshadowing the protagonist? If so, in what way?

After answering, revise to address the issues you noted before reading my revision.

Problem with original:

Jake's only purpose is to chat and hand over the coffee. If you remove him (or this scene entirely), it wouldn't change the story.

Revised:

Covey adjusted her headset and stared at the blinking cursor on her computer screen. She was supposed to submit her final project proposal by noon, but her brain felt like oatmeal.

"Still stuck?" her coworker, Jake, asked from the next cubicle. He leaned over the divider, holding his ever-present travel mug.

"Yeah," Covey said. "Can't get this section right."

"Let me guess. Your idea is solid, but you're apologizing for it."

"What do you mean?"

Jake stood up on his desk and hopped over the divider. Hopped!

"What on earth? Did you just—" Crap. He had read her latest attempt.

"Yep. All those 'maybe,' 'possibly,' 'perhaps.' Just own it. You're the one pitching it, not begging for permission. Okay? Just, you know, have some confidence instead of writing like you don't even believe your own idea."

"Wow. Brutal honesty and no offer of coffee."

He shrugged. "Look, you're the expert here. On your job, not on coffee. I think somehow the coffee tastes worse if you even touch the machine, so yeah, I'll get you some."

After he walked away, Covey stared at the screen. He wasn't wrong. She highlighted the last three paragraphs, hovered over the delete button for a second, then pressed it. The cursor blinked on top of a blank page. She cracked her knuckles and started typing again.

Now Jake serves a purpose: to challenge the MC and force her to see a personal flaw (lack of confidence) that ties into her growth arc. Plus, I gave him a bit of a personality.

EDITING STEPS

❏ Write down each side character's function in a given scene. If they lack purpose, cut them out or revise to give them one.

❏ Ensure each side character has one to three defining characteristic(s) that remain consistent throughout and that they have a life of their own.

❏ Read through scenes where side characters are prominent and ask, Is this scene ultimately about the MC's journey, even if the side character is more active? If yes, keep it. If no, revise or cut.

❏ Ensure the MC has a strong internal experience in these scenes. Are we in their head, feeling their reaction, watching them change? Or are they just a camera observing the side character?

❏ Do the side characters have their own subplot that readers get invested in that doesn't help or hinder the MC in any way? If yes, drop it entirely or shorten it and weave it into specific moments.

STOP: DON'T READ AHEAD YET

Apply the two or three topics you chose for this pass to your manuscript before moving on.

This book is a toolbox, not a linear book. You'll get the most value from doing the work *as you go*.

If you haven't done so yet, scan the QR code or visit: https://beaconpointservices.org/generate-fiction -personalized-workbook.

For best results, open on a computer or tablet to download and edit the Word document.

When you're ready, come back and begin the next pass.

You've got this.

SCENE PASS

Think of your story as a necklace: The story pass ensured the string was strong and the clasp worked (in other words, that the narrative works as a whole). Take a minute to recognize how much your editing improved your story. Now the scene pass will polish each individual bead until it catches the light (ensuring each unit delivers).

A scene that works in isolation may not work within your story, while a scene that serves your plot may still fall flat in execution. During this pass, you'll shift from asking, Does this serve my story? to Does this scene itself work?

First, remember how we defined a scene: a unit of action, unfolding in continuous time, with its own mini-story arc and a clear beginning, middle, and end. When you make a significant jump in time or location or shift character focus, you start a new scene. This definition will help you as you analyze your scenes.

I'll warn you: This pass can get intense. So don't try to fix everything at once. Choose two or three of the topics to read and apply, and only look at what you need to for that topic. You don't necessarily need to read your whole book for this pass.

If your scenes feel slow at the beginning or fizzle out at the end:

- Craft strong entry and exit points (page 104)

If your story feels choppy, rushed, or like it's "just a string of events":

- Structure with action and reaction (page 115)

If some scenes feel "nice" but not necessary, or nothing truly goes wrong:

- Build conflict and stakes (page 122)

If the big pieces are in place, but pages feel oddly flat or too smooth:

- Generate microtension (page 127)

If you're unsure what to pick, sign up to get notified when my diagnostic tool is ready or check out my Manuscript Checkup service, both in appendix A.

Personalized workbook: To generate your customizable scene pass workbook, scan the QR code or visit https://beaconpointservices.org/generate-fiction-personalized-workbook.

For best results, open on a computer or tablet to download and edit the Word document.

Craft Strong Entry and Exit Points

How often have you watched a YouTube video or listened to a podcast and thought, *Get to the point?* Speakers can easily spend too much time on the setup or drag out the conclusion, but since videos and podcasts are relatively short, the audience can more easily forgive them. In a novel, on the other hand? It just might cause the reader to close your book and never pick it up again.

The key to writing a strong scene is to start late and leave early. This means you begin the scene in the middle of the action (*in medias res*) and end it with a lingering revelation, question, setback, or cliffhanger.

Entry point

The cliché advice to "start with action" can be problematic because it's misunderstood as meaning start with intense physical action. You can't start with just any action; you need to start with the *critical* situation. Critical situations impact the plot or reveal characterization. So start there instead of with throat-clearing or fluff.

Once the throat-clearing is gone, open with the scene's purpose. If the purpose is to develop the character, begin with a situation that reveals the main character's (MC's) personality, goals, or flaws. This can be a direct action, internal thought, or dialogue. If the purpose is to advance the plot, open with a situation that creates an immediate problem or a nagging question for the reader. Regardless of the purpose, if your scene signifies a change in time and location, then you do need to include some setting and atmosphere details to ground the reader, but don't spend too long on that unless it's critical to know before the action.

Original:

> Carly pulled into the crowded parking lot, circling twice before finally finding a spot near the back. She turned off the ignition and glanced at the clock. She was late.
>
> Scrambling, she grabbed her purse, climbed out, and locked the car. The wind tugged at her coat as she walked toward the front doors of the school.
>
> [Insert exposition of wind kicking up leaves and getting them tangled in her hair. A boy on a skateboard almost running into her. Then a flashback of her time as a student at this school.]
>
> Inside, the smell of floor polish hit her, mingling with the faint scent of cafeteria pizza. She glanced down the hall. Pretty sure Mrs. Phelps's class was in this hall. If it wasn't, she would be even later than she already was.
>
> "Carly!" a voice called.
>
> She turned to see Mrs. Phelps waving her over.

The true purpose of this scene is the interaction between Carly and Mrs. Phelps, but it takes a while to get there. We have some mundane actions (parking, walking) that don't reveal anything new about her character or advance the plot. Yes, the flashback and the issues getting into the school do reveal character, but you could also just reveal that in the interaction between the characters and incorporate the flashbacks into the action.

Revised scene opening:

> "Carly, I see you still don't own a watch." Mrs. Phelps's sharp tone froze her halfway down the hall.

Not again. Carly straightened, forcing a smile as she turned. The wind-tossed leaves had done a number on her hair, but it's not like she had looked that put together even before that. Really, if Mrs. Phelps wanted her at her best, she shouldn't have insisted on a 9 a.m. appointment.

"Sorry. It's just that . . . well . . . yeah." Carly shrugged. Shrugged like a teenage kid. Stupid.

Mrs. Phelps stared at her. Long. Hard. Painful. She wasn't a student here anymore. Thank goodness. But she might as well be back in the principal's office. Principal Phelps. Yep. At least she didn't have to deal with her daily, like her current students do now that she's a teacher. Carly shivered.

Now the scene opens with the moment of conflict and reveals information about the MC's inner world.

I intentionally created a scene that opens with more internal than external action right at the start, and that's fine. Remember, *in medias res* doesn't always mean dropping us into intense action. We don't need bombs exploding or a cowboy standoff. Even though it wasn't "action-packed," this scene still started in the middle of the action. The only point of Carly being in the car, parking, and walking up to the school was to show her internal world, so I wove that world into the moment that did matter (being confronted by Mrs. Phelps) and cut out the moments that didn't.

Exit point

A good scene ends with something left unresolved, so the reader keeps reading to find out what happens next.

Since the MC (and other characters, too, as needed) should have a goal in each scene, if they end up failing at their goal—well, that's an unresolved ending right there. Ending with disaster is a great way to keep those pages turning.

Even if your character does achieve their scene goal—which they can and should sometimes—don't end the scene there. Instead, your character achieves their goal, and then bam! Another obstacle leaves the reader wondering what it means or what will happen next.

End the scene by:

- Posing a question/withholding information (mystery)
- Raising the stakes with a new conflict (escalation)
- Ending with a setback/disaster (failure)
- Ending with a shift (turning point in perspective or direction)
- Giving a partial reveal (mystery)
- Introducing a new plot twist (escalation)

The following examples show summaries of scene endings from various published novels. (Examples generated by ChatGPT; analysis is my own.)

Posing a question or withholding information:

> And then I heard the sound of the cannon (*Hunger Games* by Suzanne Collins).

> *At this point in the book, the reader knows the cannon signals death, so the scene ends with a question: Who died?*

> And then I saw what was inside the envelope. My stomach dropped (Gone Girl by Gillian Flynn).

> *All we know is that something huge has happened, but we don't know what. We're kept in ignorance of the complete revelation until the next scene.*

Raising the stakes with a new conflict:

> There was no mistaking it this time. Snape definitely hated him (*Harry Potter and the Sorcerer's Stone* by J.K. Rowling).
>
> *This scene ends by introducing a new personal conflict that deepens the stakes beyond just "surviving school."*

Ending with a shift:

> Till this moment I never knew myself (*Pride and Prejudice* by Jane Austen).
>
> *This is a profound moment of self-awareness. At this moment, the story shifts from external conflict (Elizabeth versus Mr. Darcy) to internal conflict (Elizabeth's self-growth), signaling a new phase in both the plot and the character arc.*

Self-editing in practice

Original A: Scene opening

> Julian woke up at 6:30 a.m. on the dot. After making a pot of coffee, he sat down and reviewed his lesson notes. It wasn't his best lesson, but it aligned with the Common Core, and his principal would approve. When he got to the school, he snagged a good parking spot. A good start to his day. His first class didn't go as well as he'd hoped. They were half-asleep. He tried making a joke about *The Great Gatsby* but only got two polite chuckles.
>
> By the time the lunch bell finally rang, his throat was dry and his patience thinner. He joined the flow of students and teachers heading to the cafeteria.

After getting the garlic dippers, not his favorite but not too bad, he headed to the teacher's lounge. He sat down, opened the sauce, and nodded to Greg, the history teacher.

"Got your grade reports in?" Greg asked.

"Barely. The system crashed twice," Julian said.

Greg chuckled. "Same. I swear the district servers are held together with duct tape. You coming to the faculty mixer Friday?"

"Maybe. Depends how the week goes."

Greg sighed. "Same old story." He bit into his apple. "At least it's pizza day."

Julian smiled weakly. "Living the dream."

Greg launched into a story about a student using ChatGPT to cheat again. Julian half-listened, half-scrolled through his phone. When the notification count caught his eye, he opened his email—and froze.

We need to talk about Ava.

The garlic dippers looked even less appealing.

PAUSE HERE

Open your personalized workbook on your computer and review the practice exercise, asking

- When does the *real* purpose of this scene kick in? What moment actually matters to the story?

- If you had to start this scene *later,* what's the earliest line you could cut to and still have readers feel grounded and curious?

After answering, draft a new scene beginning before reading my revision.

Problem with original:

At first glance, this might seem like an okay scene opening. It's not *bad* bad, but nothing pulls us into the scene. Julian just wakes up, makes coffee, teaches an unremarkable class, and has forgettable banter with a fellow teacher. Nothing is engaging enough to make us wonder what will happen next. And it starts three settings before the real purpose of the scene (the email): Julian's house, his classroom, the cafeteria. The story doesn't truly begin until that email appears. Everything before it is throat-clearing.

Initially, this excerpt was even longer, with a paragraph at his house, two paragraphs in the classroom, and one in the lunchroom. I shortened it for this example, but writers do stack several non-critical paragraphs or pages before the scene truly begins. The principle is the same whether you're cutting one paragraph or five pages: Start where it matters.

Revised A:

> Balancing his tray on one hand, Julian wove through the crowded room. The hum of conversation rose and fell around him, punctuated by the squeak of sneakers on tile. He spotted a few of his students huddled over their phones in the corner and gave a quick wave. None of them noticed.
>
> He'd barely sat down in the teachers' lounge when Greg launched into a story about a student using ChatGPT to cheat again. Julian half-listened, half-scrolled through his phone. When the notification count caught his eye, he opened his email—and froze.
>
> *We need to talk about Ava.*
>
> His sandwich suddenly didn't look so appealing.
>
> *I started the scene with some sensory details and a little bit of characterization. Sure, you could open with "Julian sat in the teacher's lounge,*

scrolling through his phone. When the notification caught his eye . . ." or even "We need to talk about Ava. He reread the email again and again." But the other details ground us in the scene, giving just a bit of setting and characterization while still dropping in medias res: Julian already has his food and is in the cafeteria.

Original B: Scene ending

I'll continue the same scene in this example. During his afternoon class, he keeps glancing at Ava's empty desk; her absence makes the email even more unsettling. Now it's the end of the school day.

> Julian gathered his papers and shoved them into his messenger bag. The building was already emptying out, students streaming toward the exits, teachers packing up for the day. He glanced at his phone one more time. The email sat there, unanswered.
>
> He should probably head to the office. Get it over with. Find out what this was all about.
>
> But his planning period had run late, and now it was almost 3:30. The office staff usually left by 4:00 on Wednesdays. He could go now, or he could wait until tomorrow morning when he had had time to think about it.
>
> Tomorrow made more sense. He'd be calmer then. More prepared.
>
> Julian locked his classroom door and headed for the parking lot. The autumn air was crisp, the sky already dimming. He climbed into his car, tossed his bag onto the passenger seat, and sat there for a moment.
>
> *We need to talk about Ava.*
>
> He'd deal with it in the morning. Fresh start. Clear head.
>
> He turned the key and drove home.

> ### PAUSE HERE
>
> - At the end of this scene, is anything truly unresolved, or does Julian land in a place of comfort and certainty?
>
> - What specific question, complication, or new threat could you lean into right at the end to make the reader turn the page?
>
> - Does the final beat deflate the tension or increase it (does something happen that makes waiting impossible)?
>
> After answering, determine a new way to end the scene before reading my revision.

Problems with original:

The scene ends with Julian making a decision that deflates all tension: He'll wait until tomorrow. The immediate question is resolved (he's not going to the office now). The scene just winds down into a return to normalcy. Nothing is propelling us forward into the next scene. Sure, the scene technically has an unresolved question hanging over the whole story (what's going on with Ava?), but the scene itself ends on a moment of resolution: Julian makes a decision. The scene's immediate tension is resolved even though the story's larger question remains. This makes it a weak ending.

Revised B:

Julian gathered his papers and shoved them into his messenger bag. He should head to the office. Get it over with.

But when he reached the main hallway, the office lights were already off. He checked his watch: 3:35. Oh yeah, the admin staff left early on Wednesdays. Principal Harmon would be off to a meeting with their supervisor.

Well, if it could wait until tomorrow, then it clearly wasn't a big deal; it wasn't worth all the anxiety it had given him. The principal should have given more context. Gosh, that had given him a heart attack for no reason. He turned around and had only taken two steps when Principal Harmon came around the corner.

"Julian, I'm glad I caught you. I was worried when you weren't in your classroom that you had left already. I thought you would have come down during your prep period."

"Yeah . . . sorry, I—"

"No time for small talk. This is urgent. Ava's parents have filed a formal complaint."

His stomach dropped. Complaint? About what?

He stood frozen in the hallway, the fluorescent lights humming overhead. Whatever this was, it wasn't going to wait until tomorrow.

This ending raises the stakes with new information (formal complaint, board meeting, urgent timeline) and poses immediate questions: What's the complaint about? What did he allegedly do? Instead of defusing tension by postponing the conflict, it escalates, as Julian now has less time and higher stakes.

EDITING STEPS

- ❑ Identify the purpose of the scene—introduce conflict or goal, reveal something about the point of view (POV) character, etc.—and ensure the entry point aligns with that purpose.
- ❑ Ensure you're starting *in medias res*—in the middle of the action or situation that matters.
  - Action can be internal (conflict, decision, fear) or external (dialogue, confrontation, event).
  - Don't confuse "start with action" with a full-on chaotic, action-packed scene.
  - Locate where the true action and tension begin and cut any fluff or throat-clearing that doesn't add essential plot or characterization.
  - Orient us with a few clear, concrete details if you have shifted time and location. Include just enough to set tone and context, but not so much that it delays the action.
- ❑ Read the last few lines of the scene and ask, Does this leave something unresolved? If not, revise to end with
  - a new conflict or obstacle
  - a complication to the victory just achieved
  - a decision or choice that carries consequences
  - a discovery that changes the character's understanding
  - a line of dialogue or image that hints at what's coming next
- ❑ Cut out any routine scene endings (drove home, went to bed, left the restaurant).

Structure with Action and Reaction

Have you ever binge-read a thriller that left you weirdly hollow? Or slogged through a character study that felt like watching paint dry? Both stem from the same craft mistake: an imbalance between action and reaction.

When your story feels uneven—too rushed in some places and sluggish in others—the problem often lies in how you balance action and reaction. Every story moment should either push events forward or show how your character processes what just happened. These story units are called scenes and sequels, but I find that terminology confusing since a sequel is part of a scene. So let's use the terms "action" and "reaction," which are two halves of a scene.

- Action is when something *happens*: Your character pursues a goal, faces obstacles, and encounters change.
- Reaction is when your character *responds*: They feel, think, and decide what to do next.

Together, action and reaction form the heartbeat of story momentum. It's important to note, however, that not every scene *needs* both parts. In fact, if you included both action and reaction in every single scene, your story would suffer from pacing problems.

Action

Action is your story's engine, built on goal, conflict, and outcome, and its purpose is to move the plot forward.

Goal: At the start of the scene, the protagonist wants something specific. Yes, they have an overall book goal, but they also have a smaller scene goal, what they want right now.

Conflict: Within that scene, something must get in their way.

Outcome: Did they achieve or not achieve their goal? If they did achieve it, then what can be a new outcome: twist or complication that makes the character's next move uncertain?

Example:

> Let's say the scene is a character at a job interview.
>
> Goal: Get the job.
>
> Conflict: Interview questions expose a weakness.
>
> Outcome: It's clear she failed the interview.

The "Build Conflict and Stakes" topic will discuss how to ensure you have strong conflicts in a scene, so that's all I'll say here.

Reaction

The reaction shows a character's emotional and mental fallout from what just happened and leads naturally into the next round of action. A reaction typically includes three parts: the character's reaction, the dilemma that follows, and the decision that moves them forward.

Occasionally, you need to let your character feel the hit so the reader can connect with them on a human level. Once emotions settle, your character can then assess what just happened. What did they learn? What do they now understand about themselves, their situation, or their opponent? Finally, they choose what to do next. This decision launches the next scene's goal, creating a natural rhythm of action → reaction → action.

Example:

> Now that the character has failed the interview, she needs to process it.
>
> Reaction: Experience emotional fallout (humiliation and frustration).
>
> Reflection: Realize her skills need updating.
>
> Decision: Enroll in a workshop and prepare for another chance.

After this reaction, we begin the next scene in *medias res*. We start in the middle of the workshop, where the students have been given thirty-five minutes to complete a task and our protagonist is figuring out how to do it.

And now we have a new action sequence: Her goal is to learn the skill set and close the gap (goal), but, of course, there will be conflict, which will culminate in a scene ending in a twist or complication (outcome).

Original:

> Scene 1: Doctor Elliot Vale tells Frank the cancer has spread. Frank leaves. Elliot moves on to his next patient.
>
> Scene 2: Elliot's colleague pulls him aside and tells him Frank had come to the clinic six months ago with early symptoms. The intake notes were flagged but never forwarded to Elliot.
>
> Scene 3: Elliot submits a formal request for Frank's full intake file. The records coordinator tells him the file has already been pulled by hospital administration. She doesn't know why (generated by Claude).

Scene 1 is missing a conflict. Nothing gets in Elliot's way or creates friction. Scene 3 could use a reaction component because he just experienced something unsettling.

Revised:

> In scene 1, Frank becomes angry and tells Elliot he came in six months ago, feeling terrible, and was sent home. He wants to know why nobody caught this sooner. Frank leaves before Elliot can respond.
>
> Scene 2 stays the same. In scene 3, Elliot stands in the hallway, thinking about Frank's daughter waiting in the next room and feeling the weight of what he can and can't tell her yet. He decides he'll say nothing until he knows what he's dealing with, but he's not letting it go.

Balancing the two parts

If your manuscript races from event to event without pause, readers may feel exhausted or disconnected. If it lingers too long in thought, momentum stalls. A well-paced manuscript has a good balance of action-only scenes and scenes with both action and reaction. That's right: not every scene needs a reaction, as that would be repetitive. Reaction sequences should ensure the character undergoes an emotional arc and growth, not repeat the same reactive emotion and similar reflection across multiple scenes.

The sweet spot is alternating these units in a rhythm that fits your genre and voice. Thrillers often keep reactions short and have several consecutive scenes without them. Romance and literary fiction, on the other hand, may linger longer in the emotional aftermath.

Self-editing in practice

Original:

Scene 1: Milly storms into her boss's office and quits after he takes credit for her work. Furious but empowered, she grabs her things and walks out.

Scene 2: That evening, she meets an old friend who mentions a startup that's hiring. Milly agrees to an impromptu interview that same night.

Scene 3: The founder loves her ideas and offers her a position until an urgent call interrupts, revealing the company's shady dealings. Milly storms out again, determined to start her own business (generated by Claude).

PAUSE HERE

Open your personalized workbook on your computer and review the practice exercise, asking

- For each scene, what's the goal, conflict, and outcome? Are any scenes missing any components?

- Where is a reaction lacking (no emotional fallout, no reflection, no decision after a big moment)? Where should there be one?

- What action sequences are fine without a reaction after them?

After answering, determine how you would fix these issues before reading my revision.

Problems with original:

Scene 2 lacks a conflict, and we have three action sequences back-to-back without any reaction.

Revised:

> In scene 1, add a reaction sequence where Milly sits in her car and the rush of victory fades, replaced by a hollow twist in her stomach. She questions her decision and begins panicking. But then she determines to prove him wrong.
>
> To add a conflict in scene 2, perhaps her friend tells her about this opportunity and Milly gets really giddy. He also tells her the company does have a chaotic reputation, but she keeps brushing it off. When he says something cryptic and insinuates she'll regret the interview, she second-guesses herself but decides to do it anyway.
>
> You don't need a reaction sequence between scenes 2 and 3.

EDITING STEPS

❑ If your story moves too fast, add short reflective beats after big moments (you may just need a few sentences of reaction). If your story drags, tighten or combine slower reactions so the action resumes before a reader's patience wears thin.

  • Optional idea: Color code your manuscript: one color for action sequences and another for reaction sequences. Now, zoom out and look at the color balance in your manuscript. If you have too much action or reflection in a row, weave in the missing balance.

❑ When your scene includes a reaction, make sure to include the reaction, the dilemma that follows, and the decision that moves them forward.

❑ Within your reaction sequences, ensure your character's emotions evolve. They shouldn't feel the same after every scene. If they do, the reaction sequence is just filler and should either be cut or replaced with a different reaction.

Build Conflict and Stakes

If you opted to work on establishing and escalating the central conflict in the story pass, then some of this information will be a repeat. But we're now focusing on this topic at the scene level.

You need to constantly ask two questions, because the reader will definitely be asking them: What's preventing the character from reaching their goal (that's the conflict), and what does the protagonist stand to lose if they don't (those are the stakes)? This means that every scene needs a clear goal, real obstacles, and meaningful consequences if the character fails.

This doesn't mean you need explosive action all the time. Conflict can be emotional (internal struggles) or physical (external struggles), and the emotional stakes can be just as essential or even greater than the physical ones. The best scenes often layer both: a character faces an external barrier while also wrestling with internal doubts, fears, or competing desires.

If you can't state the goal, conflict, and stake for a given scene or if it feels flat, you need to introduce a conflict and/or raise the emotional and/or physical stakes.

Start by identifying what the character wants in the scene and how they feel about it. Then you can use two proven frameworks to build the conflict and stakes: "yes, but" or "when, then, until."

"Yes, but": *Yes*, the character has a goal, *but* something is in their way, and if they don't get it, then they risk this (stake).

Example:

> *Yes*, the character wants to get home in time for the birth of his baby, *but* he also really needs to get the meth to the dealer in the next hour, or he'll lose his one opportunity to sell in bulk (Walter White in *Breaking Bad*).
>
> *He physically can't be in two places at once (external conflict), so he has to choose to prioritize either his identity as a father or a drug dealer (internal conflict).*
>
> *Stakes: Miss the birth, and he hurts his marriage; miss the deal, and he loses crucial income and credibility.*

"When, then, until" framework: "*When* the [scene] begins with this world and character, *then* this small conflict happens, *until* cliffhanger until the next [scene]."[3] The *when* of the next scene is the cliffhanger from the previous scene.

Example:

> *When* Jim and Pam arrive at Michael and Jan's painfully awkward dinner party, they plan to get through the evening quickly.
>
> *Then* Michael pressures them to stay, and Jan becomes increasingly hostile.
>
> *Until* Jan smashes a Dundie award in anger, and the scene cuts away.
>
> *They're trapped socially (external conflict) and caught between pity and discomfort (internal conflict).*
>
> *Stakes: Leave early and hurt Michael; stay and endure the chaos.*

---

3   On a handout from Julie Grey, Substantive & Developmental Editing

So let's look at how this works at the revision stage.

Original:

> Dana received a call from her mom, and her mom told her not to tell her sister. Three days later, she arrives at her sister's house for Sunday dinner. They eat and catch up about work and their kids. Before leaving, Dana's sister asks if she's okay because she seems distracted. Dana says she's fine and drives home.

> *Dana doesn't encounter any obstacles to meeting her goal (keep the news of her mother's call from her sister), and nothing seems to be at stake. Neither framework can be applied.*

Revised:

> Dana arrives at her sister's house for Sunday dinner. *When* her sister keeps bringing up their mother casually, *then* Dana's silence feels more like a lie. *Until* her sister finds the voicemail notification on Dana's phone while borrowing it to look up a recipe, and dinner goes very quiet.

Self-editing in practice

Original (summarized scene from a manuscript I edited):

> Character wakes up and helps her mom unpack, then goes out to eat with her mom. They continue unpacking, and her new friend comes over to help her decorate her new room.

> **PAUSE HERE**
>
> Open your personalized workbook on your computer and review the practice exercise, asking
>
> - In this scene, what does the character want right now, and what's standing in the way of that desire?
> - If you tried to plug the scene into either framework—"yes, but" (she wants X, *but* Y gets in the way) or "When . . . then . . . until" (when the scene starts like this, then this complication happens, until this new cliffhanger)—where does it fall apart?
> - What would be at stake emotionally or practically if this scene went differently, or if it didn't exist at all?
>
> After answering, revise the scene to increase the conflict and stakes before reading my revision.

Problem with original:

This scene establishes the MC's personality and her relationships with her mom and friend, but nothing happens. Neither framework can be applied to this scene.

Revised (two ideas):

- When, then, until: When the scene begins, this character is bantering with her mom despite hating that they're moving again, then she discovers her most treasured box didn't arrive, and without it, she can't feel settled into her room, which is what she has always needed to be okay with moving yet again. She'll be angry at her mom and at her unfair life as an Army brat until it arrives.
- Yes, but: Her new friend comes over to help her unpack, and that's great, but then her best friend from her old house calls. She wants to talk to her best friend, but she doesn't want to ditch her new friend.

EDITING STEPS

❑ Chart the goal, conflict, and stake for every scene or just those that feel flat.

❑ For those that don't have a clear conflict and/or stakes, revise the scene using a "yes, but" or "when, then, until" framework.

Generate Microtension

You know that sensation when you're reading and you can't quite relax, even during a quiet scene? That low-level unease that keeps you glued to the page? That's microtension, and without it, even your most dramatic scenes will fall flat.

Microtension keeps readers emotionally present in the scene.[4] It's the moment-to-moment unease, the emotional friction. In other words, while the conflict and stakes define the scene's obstacle and *why* it matters, the microtension defines *how* it feels while it's happening.

For example, if your scene is a character in a job interview, the main goal is to get the job, and the conflict could be that the interviewer's unexpected questions expose the character's weaknesses. And then the microtension gives us the emotional beats moment by moment:

- She forces a smile but knows her palms are slick with sweat.
- The interviewer's kind tone clashes with his sharp questions.
- She laughs too loudly after a joke that wasn't funny.
- A voice in her head whispers she's ruining her one chance.

To create microtension, ask, What does this character want right now, and what's keeping them from getting it? I know this sounds similar to the questions we ask to establish conflict, but conflict is different than microtension.

---

4   I used AI to initially draft this topic, as I had just recently learned about it, then I added to it extensively and revised the output to make it my own.

> **Clarification: Conflict versus microtension**
>
> Conflict shapes what's happening in the scene; microtension shapes how the moment *feels* as the character moves through it.

To create microtension, try these tactics:

- Cause something to feel slightly off—body language that doesn't match dialogue, a pause too long, an unspoken thought that shifts the tone.
- Include references to something in the past (this morning, years ago, whatever) that gets the reader curious.
- Have characters act and speak in ways that contradict their goals and desires.
- Have characters misinterpret their own emotions.
- Let conflicting emotions sit side by side (e.g., pride under fear, affection under anger. Readers can sense that complexity even if you never name it. This is the best way to create microtension. Find those secondary emotions.)
- Allow a character's emotional state to influence how they perceive and describe their surroundings.
- Create dialogue exchanges with contradictory ideas and needs, interruptions, clipped responses, or silence.
- Hint at deeper, unspoken feelings beneath the surface of the conversation.
- Describe the setting in a way that builds tension.
- Have the setting and scene be contradictory to the character's mood.
- Make one character uncertain or suspicious of the other.

You can use more than one tactic in a given scene, as microtension is moment to moment.

Original:

Tariq said, "I'm not angry," and went back to eating his food.

Revised:

Tariq said, "I'm not angry." He stabbed his steak and cut it into smaller and smaller pieces until his knife had nowhere to go.

Now we have body language that doesn't match the dialogue.

Original:

"It's official, Mom. I dropped out of college, and I'm touring with my band."

Renata smiled.

Revised:

Renata smiled. A genuine smile. Her son, a successful musician? Under the table she pressed her thumbnail into her palm until she felt it.

Now we have conflicting emotions

Original:

David sat in the hospital waiting room.

Revised:

> David sat in the waiting room. Someone nearby was eating chips, the crinkle of the bag loud and steady, and he couldn't stop counting the seconds between each one.

Now we have sensory details showing the emotion.

Self-editing in practice

Since this concept happens moment to moment, it's hard to show in a short practice exercise, but the following example should give you at least a taste of the concept. (Side note: I chatted with Claude for a good forty-five minutes, trying to refine the examples it gave me because the first nine iterations weren't working.)

Original:

> Scene overview: Lila, a young archaeologist, must retrieve a fragile artifact before a storm hits. Her mentor has warned her not to go alone, but she's determined to prove she can handle the dig herself.
>
> Lila reached the dig site and began brushing sand from the stone tablet. The wind picked up, blowing grit into her face. She worked faster, checking the sky. Thunder rumbled in the distance. She packed the tablet into a crate and carried it toward the truck. The first drops of rain hit as she climbed in and drove away.
>
> The rain pounded harder as she bumped along the dirt road back toward camp. When she reached the supply tent, she unloaded the crate and checked the tablet for cracks. It was intact—thankfully. She covered it with a tarp and exhaled, finally letting her shoulders drop.

She'd done it. Against the odds, she'd saved the find. Dr. Niles would now have to admit she was ready for a solo assignment. Just then, she saw a scratch on the tablet (generated by Claude).

PAUSE HERE

Open your personalized workbook on your computer and review the practice exercise, asking

- Does the character's emotional state noticeably shift as the scene unfolds?
- Where could you add a contradictory beat?
- If you highlighted only her interior reactions, would you see a progression or mostly repetition?

After answering, revise the scene to add microtension before reading my revision.

Problem with original:

This scene works perfectly on a structural level. She has a goal (retrieve the artifact before the storm), a conflict (the worsening weather and her mentor's disapproval), and a strong scene ending with outcome (a revelation of the scratch). But it's emotionally flat. The obstacle resolves too smoothly, and her emotions don't change.

Revised:

The storm would miss them like it always did. It had to. She had told herself that this morning. And now, standing at the dig site, a light was seeping through the gray. That was a good sign. Had to be a good sign.

The wind scraped sand across the half-buried tablet. She brushed carefully, but her hand kept slipping. *Too fast*, she scolded herself.

You'll crack it. When a gust lifted the corner of the tarp, she scrambled to catch it with her knee, heart hammering.

Dr. Niles's voice pounded in her head as clearly as if he was standing behind her: *No solo work. You make mistakes when you rush.*

He might be right.

She brushed more slowly. She could do it. A few more brushes and the sand would give her what was hers.

The first drop hit the back of her neck—cold, sharp. It didn't matter. Nothing did. She had it. She had the tablet. She wrapped it in canvas, cinched the twine, and lifted it against her chest. The wind shoved her sideways. Her boot slid on the embankment, and she stopped breathing. If she lost her balance and dropped the artifact, she would lose everything, just like she did five years ago. No, she couldn't think about that now. She righted herself. Breathing in and out, she hugged the tablet to her chest. She shivered, and not just from the cold.

Hail began pounding against her coat. She laughed. A loud, wild laugh. She'd done it. He'd have to promote her now. The hail hit her exposed hand, then her head. But it didn't matter. Her sister should see her now, standing in the middle of a hailstorm. Well, she wasn't whining about the cold anymore.

By the time she reached the truck, the hail had grown in size. She slammed the door, panting, the tablet in her lap.

She reached for her phone, thumb hovering over Dr. Niles's number, then dropped it again when lightning flashed. When she turned to pick it up, her heart sank. With her phone glowing, she saw it. This could end her.

I added in contradictory thoughts (he might be right) and conflicting emotions (confident, full of pride, but also scared and unsure of herself). Then I used the setting to raise the tension and had her tell herself lies, like the storm would pass them by. The environment contradicted her mood (she was laughing despite the hail). And I dropped in some references to her past.

EDITING STEPS

Note: If a scene isn't structurally sound, that should be your focus before worrying about microtension.

❑ If a scene is structurally sound with a goal, conflict, stakes, and a scene ending that leaves the reader wanting more, but the scene itself feels flat, add in microtension, using a few different tactics:
  • Something feels off: body language that doesn't match dialogue, a pause too long, an unspoken thought that shifts the tone
  • References to something in the past (this morning, years ago, whatever) that get the reader curious and wondering
  • Characters acting and speaking in ways that contradict their goals and desires
  • Characters misinterpreting their own emotions
  • Characters with conflicting emotions: pride under fear, affection under anger
  • A character's emotional state influencing how they perceive and describe their surroundings
  • Conversations containing interruptions, clipped responses, contradictory ideas, or silence
  • Setting described in a way that builds tension
  • Setting and scene that contradict the character's mood
  • One character being uncertain or suspicious of the other

STOP: DON'T READ AHEAD YET

Apply the two or three topics you chose for this pass to your manuscript before moving on.

This book is a toolbox, not a linear book. You'll get the most value from doing the work as you go.

If you haven't done so yet, scan the QR code or visit: https://beaconpointservices.org/generate-fiction -personalized-workbook.

For best results, open on a computer or tablet to download and edit the Word document.

When you're ready, come back and begin the next pass.

You've got this.

WRITING PASS

Woo-hoo! Your scenes sing now. Take a minute to reflect on how much stronger your book is because you edited at the scene level. You're almost there. You have just a little bit to go to help your reader by improving the writing. I rarely stop reading a book because the story is weak. It just gets a lower rating from me, but I still finish it. When I abandon a novel, it's because the writing pulled me out of the experience—too much telling, weak wording and sentence structure, shallow interiority, or dialogue that doesn't sound like real people talking.

Many of those books have solid premises and compelling characters. But when the writing creates distance instead of immersion, I can't stay in the world long enough to care. This pass is where that disconnect gets fixed. After all, plot, character, tension, and emotion all reach the reader through the writing itself. A strong story can survive imperfect sentences, but it can't fully connect through them.

I have broken this pass into two overarching categories: narrative techniques and words and sentences. Narrative techniques are writing tools that shape how you tell the story (elements like showing versus telling and interiority), while words and sentences ensure your writing is sharp, clear, and not monotonous. You might have a strong narrative voice (technique) that's being undermined by cluttered sentences (words and sentences) or have crisp sentences (words and sentences) that lack atmospheric depth (technique).

This pass is the longest, so it's especially important not to attempt everything. I suggest you choose three topics for this one. If you're unsure what to pick, sign up to get notified when my diagnostic tool is ready or check out my Manuscript Checkup service, both in appendix A.

But in general, if your prose feels flat, distant, or explanatory:

- Master show and tell (page 163)
- Deepen interiority and close narrative distance (page 139)

If your chapters stall for backstory or worldbuilding:

- Craft effective exposition (avoid info dumping) (page 175)

If readers don't know whose head they're in:

- Ensure point of view consistency (avoid head hopping) (page 157)

If your dialogue feels wooden, overly formal, or identical across characters:

- Strengthen dialogue (page 191)

If you don't know the difference between tags and beats, or the dialogue exchanges read like talking heads:

- Refine tags and beats (page 203)

If scenes feel overwritten because you keep explaining motivations or outcomes:

- Delete unnecessary explanations (page 183)

If the writing is technically fine but doesn't sparkle:

- Strengthen word choice (page 220)
- Ensure good sentence fluency (page 230)
- Eliminate excess "be" verbs (page 241)

Personalized workbook: To generate your customizable writing pass workbook, scan the QR code or visit https://beaconpointservices.org/generate-fiction-personalized-workbook.

For best results, open on a computer or tablet to download and edit the Word document.

Narrative Techniques

Deepen Interiority and Close the Narrative Distance

Think about watching a movie. Sometimes the camera zooms in on a character's face, and you feel what they're feeling. Other times, the camera pulls back to show the whole room, and you observe from a distance. Narrative distance works the same way in writing: It's how close or far the reader feels from your character's experience.

This topic is one of the most transformative in the entire writing pass. If your pages ever feel flat, distant, or emotionally muted, interiority and narrative distance are the fix.

With a close narrative distance, you feel more connected to the point of view (POV) character, and with a wide one, you're further removed from the character.

Important note: If you're writing from the omniscient point of view, then this topic applies differently. But authors who are writing from a POV other than omniscient, more often than not, stay at too wide a distance.

A common related problem is a lack of character interiority, which is the inner life of the character. When you deepen interiority, you naturally close the narrative distance. While interiority and narrative distance are different concepts, they work hand in hand, which is why I have put them together in this topic.

Interiority = what's happening inside the character.

Narrative distance = how closely readers access and experience the interiority.

The spectrum

Take a look at the following spectrum and how it affects interiority in both first- and third-person perspectives.

In third person:

Widest distance: A woman rushed into the office building as hail pelted her.

We know nothing about the character. Seems to be an omniscient narrator telling what's happening.

Not-as-wide distance: A woman, looking haggard, closed her car door and rushed into the office as the hail beat down on her.

Now the narrator comments on the character (she looks haggard).

Medium narrow distance: Kayla Ernestine rushed into the office building. Another day at a job she hated.

We now know the character's name and a detail about her experience (she hates her job). We have been told a bit about her inner world, but not enough to be true interiority.

Narrow distance: Of course it was hailing again. Why did she stay in this horrible city and this unfulfilling job? She knew why. But still. Why? Even the door into the office posed another obstacle. The damn door should just open with a keycard or a code. But, nope, multiple times a day, she struggled with the door.

We're now in the character's thoughts, expressed in her voice. This is called free indirect speech (her words in third person as the narrator).

In first person:

While first person is inherently more intimate, given that the whole story is told from the character's perspective, you still have a spectrum of narrative distance.

Widest distance: Decades ago, a seed was planted that would change the lives of many.

We know nothing about the first-person character in this statement.

Medium distance: My mom told us the story of the magical seed that was planted decades ago. I marveled at the seed, at the possibilities it provided. I often thought of who would unlock its final powers.

We know a little about the character's interiority—what she thinks and how she reacts to the story—but these thoughts and feelings are told, not shown.

Narrow distance: Wide-eyed, I listened to my mom tell the story of the magical seed. Love and gratitude pulsed through my veins as my siblings smiled. This seed had saved them. But it could do even more. More? I shook my head and let out a laugh. Someone out there could unlock it. Probably Anitra. She certainly was good, maybe too good, and showed strength of character. It wasn't me. It was never me. I didn't even get saved by the seed. Maybe I could become worthy. Ha! Who am I kidding? Being perfect sucks, like draining-your-soul suck.

We're inside the character's thoughts, expressed in her voice.

When to go wide and when to close the distance

You may want to go wide when you're

Setting the scene: If you just want to set the scene and don't need to develop the character at that moment, it's fine to go wide. Perhaps our character feels nothing about the hail and likes her job (or her dislike has already been established or will be later). In this case, it's fine to just say, "Kayla rushed into the office building as the hail beat down on her."

Stating needed information: In a first-person story, not every scene and detail needs to be recounted through the character's voice and inner feelings. You can state the needed information, such as "My mom told us the story of the magical seed that was planted decades ago. I marveled at the seed, at the possibilities it provided. I often thought of who would unlock its final powers."

Wanting to keep the focus on the action instead of the characters: Perhaps you have a scene with a physical fight between two characters. For the first segment (the initial swing and punches), you may just describe the physical action. Then, as you move into the next segment of the fight, the POV character can express their thoughts and feelings. Or you may choose to stay wide for the entire fight scene and give the feelings afterward.

Describing a situation outside the character's understanding and vocabulary: If your POV character is a child or uneducated or doesn't have the life experience to understand the situation, you can use a wide narrative distance to detail the situation.

But outside of these situations, unless you have a reason to write the majority of your story at a wider distance (e.g., *Little Fires Everywhere*), you'll want to close the distance the majority of the time.

Techniques for closing the distance

You can quickly close the narrative distance by removing filter words and using the character's voice to color the narration.

REMOVE FILTER WORDS

When you use filter words, you're reporting. But in real life, people don't report their thoughts and feelings. They just *have* those thoughts and feelings. So reporting widens the distance.

Filter words are words like

- wondered
- realized
- hoped
- decided
- knew
- to (when used to show a character's motivation)
- because (when used to show a character's motivation)
- heard
- saw
- felt
- smelled
- tasted

Use the following examples to guide you in removing filter words.

Original A:

Phillipe **realized** he'd forgotten his tool belt.

Revised A:

Phillipe reached for his tool belt. Crap! How could he forget that?

Used free indirect speech to get rid of the filter word (I will talk about this craft tool later in this topic).

Original B:

Carly stood in front of her **to prevent her from leaving**.

Revised B:

Carly stood between Lily and the door, shaking her head.

Original C:

She woke up when she **heard** the robins singing outside her window. Delighted, she threw open the window and **saw** the smallest bird look right at her. It cocked its head to the side. She reached out her hand and gently **felt** the soft tufts of fluff.

Revised C:

The robins cheerfully whistled, waking her from her sleep. Delighted, she threw open the window. The smallest bird looked right at her, cocking its head to the side. She reached out her hand. She smiled when the soft tufts of fluff tickled her fingertips.

The rewrite still needs some work, but I purposely only removed the filter words to show the difference.

USE CHARACTER'S VOICE IN NARRATION

You can use the character's voice in the narration to close the narrative distance. Let's say we have a character, Malik, who's a relatively recent college grad of average intelligence but good at manipulation. He betrayed his former roommate Cliff but blames Cliff for it.

Original:

> Cliff sat alone at a corner table, posture languid with a laptop in front of him. His dark hair obscured his eyes as he intermittently hit a key, pausing to partake of his coffee. He wore a faded Nirvana T-shirt. A backpack leaned against his chair, and textbooks were scattered across the small table.

Here we have a generic narrator. None of this sounds like Malik. This is completely fine, but if you want to close the distance, you need to use Malik's voice.

Revised:

> Cliff was camped out at a corner table, slouched over his laptop like always. His stupid shaggy hair hung in his face while he pecked at the keys with two fingers, stopping every few minutes to drink his coffee. He'd spread his crap out all over the tiny table like he owned the place.

Now the narration takes on Malik's voice. The rewrite shows he's personally familiar with Cliff, isn't overly sophisticated in his word choice, and has some irritation toward his roommate. I removed the mention of clothes; perhaps Malik is so focused on the annoying details that he wouldn't notice the clothes. Using the character's voice also means including details the character would mention and observe.

The third and most powerful way to close the distance is to deepen the interiority. Since this involves several techniques, I gave it its own subsection below.

Deepen the interiority

I was hired by a *Wall Street Journal* bestselling author specifically to help his readers connect more with his characters. To do this, I focused on interiority, inserting the character's thoughts and feelings at various points throughout the book and shifting some of the narration into free indirect speech.

Original:

> She'd managed to make it through the session without crying, but the tears wouldn't stay held back forever.

This passage doesn't reveal any interiority. We don't really know how the character felt about the session.

Revised:

> Another "successful" session. Whatever. At least she still hadn't cried in front of the doctor. That was success in her book.

I added her thoughts to show her emotions.

HOW TO ADD INTERIORITY

Your character's internal world comes through their thoughts and emotions. You can write thoughts in three ways: directly reported, indirectly reported, or through free indirect speech.

- Direct thoughts can mean the character says their thoughts in dialogue: "Sorry. I keep forgetting practice. I feel awful." Alternatively, the thoughts can stay as thoughts and be labeled as such, either through italics or saying "thought": *Crap. I forgot practice. I feel awful.*

- Indirectly reported means the narrator is reporting the character's thoughts: Ray kept forgetting about practice despite feeling awful about it.

- Free indirect speech is a character's thoughts coming into the narration. No italics or thought tags are needed because the thoughts stay in the same form as the narration, third-person past: Crap! He forgot practice again. Of course, he felt awful but doubted the guys believed him.

In first-person stories, you can also use direct thoughts without italics or thought tags since the character is the narrator: Crap! I always forget practice. I feel awful but doubt the guys believe me.

While all three methods reveal interiority, free indirect speech or first-person direct thoughts closes the narrative distance the most.

Example using direct thoughts and free indirect speech:

> They called her name. It was her name, but it shouldn't be her name. She wasn't that name. *Stand up, Zola. I'm Zola. I'm calm.* Keeping her gaze forward, she walked up the classroom aisle. But Zola was gone. Calm was gone. The little girl with braids, always holding her teddy, was gone.
>
> Her teddy. Focus on her teddy. That's what he had said to do: Envision teddy while looking above their heads at the wall. Now that she was at the front, all she had to do was turn around. *It's just kids in a classroom.*

She jerked around and licked her dry lips. "I w-w-will t-t-talk about Af-f-fric-c-ca." Fred snickered. It had to be Fred. Don't look. Eyes on the wall. But he snickered again, and she looked. At least he couldn't see the effect it had on her, not like Noella. Her skin was so fair it betrayed her every time. Noella. Forget teddy. Dr. Kazinata was wrong. She didn't need to find Zola again. She needed to be Noella.

Her next few sentences came out easily, and she relaxed her shoulders. It was easy to talk about what she loved. "It's home to the second largest jungle, the Con—" A gunshot ricocheted off the trees. She closed her eyes. That sound. The worst sound. They'd found her. Someone screamed. Not someone. Her.

"Zola, open your eyes. You'll see you're okay." The hand on her shoulder wasn't a kadogos. Too big. Too kind. She opened her eyes. Little soldiers everywhere. They were just kids, but killers nonetheless. Kofi had been a kid. A kid with a gun. She ran.

The pitfall with thoughts is you need to make them realistic, like how humans actually think. For example, it isn't realistic for your character to think too much in question form. Sure, we all sometimes think things like, *What on earth was he thinking?* But we don't typically ask ourselves questions in our thoughts. If you resort to questions, it can read like the character is talking to the reader rather than thinking to themselves. So use questions sparingly. (Unless, of course, your character *does* question themselves in their thoughts. That would be a very unique attribute, however, and wouldn't be realistic for just any character.)

It's also unrealistic when a character thinks about things they already know and wouldn't naturally think about in that moment. This commonly shows up when a character is thinking about the "why." Why they're doing what they're doing, why their house and/or yard was designed the way it was, why their town imposed a new curfew, why they struggle with something, etc. The character already knows these things, so the only purpose for including those thoughts is to reveal the why to the reader. But that's ineffective. You can deliver the information without unrealistic thoughts.

Original:

> I had no choice except to betray him when Morrison went under, and we were facing bankruptcy. Why did Cliff want to work with the creditors? Why couldn't he just realize that was a bad idea?
>
> I know he trusts the world and the system too much. So I did the right thing by making those fake invoices.
>
> What if he recognizes me? What if Henderson finds out the truth?
>
> *These thoughts sound more like the author trying to give the reader information. It isn't natural for Malik to think in so many questions and to think about why he did what he did.*

Revised:

> Fifty thousand dollars down the drain, and Cliff had wanted to negotiate payment plans like some kind of saint.
>
> Five years of careful construction, and it could all crumble in one conversation. All Cliff has to do is mention the fake invoices.
>
> *I revised to make the thoughts feel more natural, including only what Malik would think about in that moment.*

As I mentioned before, emotions are also a part of interiority. When authors want to reveal a character's emotions through showing rather than telling, they often use physical action beats: shoulders slumped, fists clenched, etc. And that works. But emotions come from thoughts, and the reader can be made to feel the emotion more when they're invited into the character's internal world.

Let's go back to when Malik first sees Cliff at the café. Right after he describes his stupid shaggy hair and the way he has his crap spread out on the table, we want to show Malik's emotions.

Original:

> His breath caught in his throat. He took a step backward toward the door, then stopped. His hands clenched into fists at his sides. Sweat beaded on his forehead despite the air conditioning. He forced his feet forward, each step deliberate and measured. Keeping his gaze locked on Cliff, he moved toward an empty spot on the opposite side of the room. He sat down and threw the salt shaker.

All of Malik's emotions are shown through physical action beats.

Revised:

> Of course he's here.
>
> Henderson would be here in twenty minutes, expecting to find his reliable business partner, not some fraud whose past just walked back into his life.
>
> Cliff could destroy everything. Stupid Cliff. Did he have any idea what his stupid, naive faith in people had forced Malik to become? *Oh god!* He was going to look up. Malik had to move to the opposite corner now.

Now I showed his emotions through his thoughts.

WHEN TO USE INTERIORITY

Using interiority shines a spotlight on a specific moment, so use it for

- major turning points
- instances of character change
- events that alter the character's goal, motivation, or need
- moments that establish who the character is in their past, present, or expected future
- moments where characterization and theme intersect

It's also a great way to fix info dumping (see the info dumping topic on page 175). Using interiority also highlights when the words contradict the character's real thoughts.

Example:

> "Good, good. So I have been thinking more about that expansion in the Northwest market."
>
> *Crap. Portland. He's talking about Portland.* "Oh, yes, I think that is an excellent idea. How can I help?"

The interiority shows that his words do not match up to his actual thoughts.

DON'T OVERDO INTERIORITY

A word of caution: We don't need to know everything a character is thinking. After all, the average person has more than six thousand thoughts a day. If you overdo the interiority, the story slows to a crawl. You'll be constantly interrupting the action with internal commentary, and readers will lose interest.

So focus on the areas mentioned in the previous list when you want to use interiority. Make sure the interiority reveals something crucial and isn't just a repeat of earlier interiority or of what's been said externally. And unless it's crucial, don't include long sections of interiority. We don't want to read about a character just sitting and thinking, especially if they're reflecting on their past. We want forward momentum.

To ensure a good balance, you want the action that caused the character's thoughts and feelings to get more page time than the interiority.

Self-editing in practice

Use the following character information sketch to close the narrative distance and deepen interiority.

Character: Maya has been taking care of her younger brother since her parents died three years ago. She's protective but the tough-love type, tends to use dark humor as a coping mechanism, speaks in practical/ working-class language, and always puts others' needs before her own. She's scrappy and resourceful, but she struggles to ask for help.

Original:

> Maya looked at herself in the bathroom mirror and saw that her outfit was wrinkled from being stuffed into her locker and reeked of grease. She felt frustrated because she wanted to look nice for Danny's graduation, but she had no time to go home in between her shift and the graduation, so she thought bringing her outfit with her was the perfect solution.
>
> Maya had been working double shifts at the diner for the past month to save up extra money for Danny's graduation celebration. Tony's Diner was downtown, in a converted gas station, with cracked vinyl booths and fluorescent lights that flickered constantly. The smell of grease and burned coffee seemed to cling to everything, including Maya's clothes and hair. Most of the customers were truckers, construction workers, and late-night regulars who left small tips and made crude comments. The pay

was terrible, but it was steady work, and Tony let her pick up extra hours whenever she needed them.

She heard her phone ring and saw that it was Danny calling.

"Maya! Are you coming? The ceremony starts in an hour!"

She could hear the excitement in his voice when she answered. Maya felt a mix of pride and exhaustion. She forced herself to sound upbeat. "Of course I'm coming. I'm just finishing up, and then I'll head over."

She noticed that her hands were shaking slightly as she tried to fix her hair. Her shoulders ached from carrying heavy trays all night, and she felt her eyes burning from lack of sleep. She'd only gotten three hours of sleep after her shift ended at 2 a.m.

"I can't wait for you to see me walk across that stage."

"Me too, kid. This is your day."

"Sorry your boss was a jerk about leaving a bit early."

"Don't you even think about that."

Maya felt her chest swell with emotion but also felt worried about how tired she looked. She tried to smile even though he couldn't see her (generated by ChatGPT).

> ## PAUSE HERE
>
> Open your personalized workbook on your computer and review the practice exercise, asking
>
> - Where is the narrator "reporting" instead of experiencing the scene?
> - How can this moment be colored by the character's voice, worldview, humor, or attitude?
> - Where could a direct thought, indirect thought, or free indirect speech reveal emotion more authentically?
> - Does the character overthink? Underthink? Think in unrealistic ways?
> - Where could you cut interiority because it's too much?
>
> After answering, revise the scene to add more interiority and close the narrative distance before reading my revision.

Problems with original:

In the moments when we do get Maya's thoughts and emotions, we're just being told about them, keeping the reader at a wider narrative distance. It reads like she's reporting on what happened rather than immersing us in the scene with her because it lacks interiority.

Revised:

Maya looked at herself in Tony's cracked bathroom mirror. Her outfit was wrinkled and reeked of grease. *Great. I look like I crawled out of a dumpster.* Danny wouldn't be first, anyway. She could have gone home to change and been a little late instead of stuffing her nice outfit in her locker while she worked.

Age twenty-six and working at a stupid, greasy food joint nights and weekends. She needed that promotion at her real job so she could quit this one. The diner's fluorescent lights buzzed overhead like angry wasps, casting everything in that sickly yellow glow that made everyone look half-dead. Which wasn't far from the truth for most of Tony's customers—truckers hopped-up on caffeine, construction guys nursing hangovers, and the usual collection of insomniacs who treated the place like their personal therapy session. Her phone rang. Danny's name lit up the screen.

"Maya! Are you coming? The ceremony starts in an hour!"

The kid practically vibrated through the phone. After three years of watching him stress over grades, college applications, and whether they could afford his cap and gown, knowing he was graduating was worth every blister on her feet. "Of course I'm coming. I'm just finishing up, and then I'll head over."

"I can't wait for you to see me walk across that stage."

"Me too, kid. This is your day."

"Sorry your boss was a jerk about leaving a bit early."

"Don't you even think about that."

Maya slumped in the break room chair. Their parents should be here for this. They should be the ones scrambling to get off work, worrying about whether they looked presentable. But it was just her, and she'd be damned if she let Danny down.

I removed all but one filter word and added interiority as both direct italicized thoughts and free indirect speech. I changed the narration to be in her voice and deleted some interiority that was overkill.

EDITING STEPS

❏ Use Word's Find feature to find filter words and remove them unless they aren't creating a distance or you're intentionally creating a wider distance.

❏ Identify scenes/moments when you want to close the distance and change the narration to reflect the character's voice: their reactions, vocabulary, attitudes, and what they would notice and care about.

❏ Identify scenes/moments that need deeper interiority and add in some.

- Use either free indirect speech, indirect thoughts, or direct thoughts as needed, knowing that free indirect speech closes the narrative distance the most.

- Make sure you don't overdo it and give us too much of the character's internal world.

- Make sure the thoughts are realistic and not just dumping information.

- Change some action beats showing character's emotions to thoughts instead.

Ensure Point of View Consistency (Avoid Head Hopping)

Head hopping occurs when you don't maintain the point of view (POV) and instead bounce around from one character's perspective to another, revealing the inner thoughts and feelings of multiple characters, without a proper scene break or clear signal.

Since head hopping causes the reader to wonder which character they should identify with, they are pulled out of the experience.

Example:

> "Swing. Yay swing," Brandon said, running toward the playground. Kimball looked at his younger brother running off, sighed, and gave in to his fate: pushing Brandon on the swing forever. *Why can't my brother enjoy the slide more? There goes my idea of working on some homework.*
>
> When Brandon reached the swing, he climbed in and smirked. There, he could at least climb up. Looking expectantly at Kimball, he said, "Underdog." Then he closed his eyes and waited, envisioning going high like Superman and making all the kids jealous. When it didn't happen, he opened his eyes and said again, "Underdog."
>
> Kimball knew his brother just wanted to feel normal, so he smiled and said, "You got it, kid!"

At the start of the scene, we're in Kimball's thoughts, seeing the scene from his perspective. Then we see it from Brandon's—he's proud of climbing onto the swing and envisions flying—and then we're back to Kimball's.

Here, POV becomes a matter of consistency rather than choosing your POV character.

Switching perspectives correctly

Now this isn't to say you have to stay in the same perspective for the whole book, but for the most part, you *should* stay in the same character's perspective for any given scene or chapter. And when you do switch perspectives, you need a clear signal.

Occasionally, some scenes are better with a perspective switch. In that case, make sure it's a longer scene and the switch is marked.

Example of switching correctly:

> Let's say we have a scene where a guy, Phillipe, storms into a family's house while they're having dinner.
>
> Since the author wants the reader to feel the family's fear, the scene opens from the father's perspective. From his perspective, we read about Phillipe stumbling in, the dialogue that ensues, and all that initially occurs for several pages. But then, when the family realizes the guy is harmless, the author has a clear signal *** and switches to Phillipe's perspective as he sits down and joins them for dinner.

Correcting it

You can correct head hopping by either deleting the information the character wouldn't know or reframing it from the character's perspective. If it's essential to the plot or developing the character, look to reframe the information. For example, a character's reaction to the POV character could be important and require a reframe. But if the information is not advancing the plot or revealing information about the POV character, delete it.

Original:

> Jim reassured his boss that it wasn't Pam. The thought of shy Pam doing anything that outrageous almost caused him to laugh. But he dutifully took the sworn statement to Pam's desk. *Gosh, she's beautiful.* Pam took the clipboard, and with shaking hands, she signed her name. Reassuring herself that there was no way they could connect it to her son, she willed her heart to stay still. She hoped Jim didn't see her shaking hands and jump to the wrong conclusion. Jim took the clipboard, walked over to his boss, and said, "There. Are you happy?"

Jim is our POV character, but we then get thoughts from Pam, which Jim wouldn't be able to report. So this scene contains head hopping.

Revised by deleting information the POV character wouldn't know:

> Jim reassured his boss it wasn't Pam. The thought of shy Pam doing anything that outrageous almost caused him to laugh. But he dutifully took the sworn statement to Pam's desk. *Gosh, she's beautiful.*
>
> Pam took the clipboard and signed her name.
>
> Jim took the clipboard, walked over to his boss, and said, "There. Are you happy?"

Revised by reframing:

Jim reassured his boss it wasn't Pam. The thought of shy Pam doing anything that outrageous almost caused him to laugh. But he dutifully took the sworn statement to Pam's desk. *Gosh, she's beautiful.*

Pam took the clipboard, **and her hands began to shake. Covering her hand with his, Jim said, "Don't worry. We all know you didn't do it."**

Pam looked up at him, wide-eyed and panicked.

"Ignore him and just breathe." Jim took the clipboard, walked over to his boss, and said, "There. Are you happy?"

Instead of Pam "willing her heart to stay still," she's showing her emotion in a way that Jim could report.

Self-editing in practice

Original:

Claire tightened her grip on the steering wheel as the rain pounded the windshield. She couldn't afford to be late—today of all days.

The wipers thudded in a steady rhythm. Beside her, Jorge sat silent, but guilt pressed on his chest. He hadn't meant to miss the exit, and he dreaded the way she would lash out once the car stopped.

Claire's heart thudded harder. The interview panel was probably checking their watches, already irritated with her. If she failed this opportunity, it would be because Jorge couldn't read a simple road sign (generated by ChatGPT).

> ## PAUSE HERE
>
> Open your personalized workbook on your computer and review the practice exercise, asking
>
> - Which thoughts or emotions belong to a character other than the POV character?
> - Which sentences report something the POV character cannot know?
> - If a non-POV insight *is* important, how could the POV character interpret it externally?
>
> After answering, eliminate or reframe any head hopping before reading my revision.

Problems with original:

Claire, as the POV character, wouldn't know that Jorge is feeling guilty for missing the exit. She could report on his actions that suggest he feels this way, but we can't actually be in his head.

Revised:

> Claire tightened her grip on the steering wheel as the rain pounded the windshield. She couldn't afford to be late—today of all days.
>
> The wipers thudded in a steady rhythm. Beside her, **Jorge kept silent, shifting in his seat. She had no time to deal with him now, but the tension made her heart thud faster.**
>
> The interview panel was probably checking their watches, already irritated with her. If she failed this opportunity, it would be because Jorge couldn't read a simple road sign.

I revised so Jorge performs an action to indicate guilt, and then we have Claire's thoughts rather than Jorge's.

EDITING STEPS

- ❑ Identify the POV character for each scene.
- ❑ Look for thoughts, emotions, and sensations attributed to any character that the POV character wouldn't realistically know.
- ❑ Decide what to do with that information.
  - If the information that comes through head hopping doesn't advance the plot, deepen the POV character, or enhance understanding of the scene, you can delete it.
  - If the head hopping is important, show it through the POV character's observations, interpretations, or reactions.

Master Show and Tell

Notice how I called this topic "Master Show *and* Tell," not "Master Show, *Don't* Tell." Sometimes you do need to tell. But for this guide, I want to focus on fixing told prose. If you want a deeper dive into when telling works, I cover that in a blog in my show and tell series.

> **Additional resource**
>
> This is a huge topic. I highly recommend Janice Hardy's book, *Understanding Show, Don't Tell: And Really Getting It*, to examine it in greater depth.[5]

To change your told prose, first you have to find it. Some told prose is really easy to spot: "he said with a tone of defeat." This clearly tells the reader about the character's emotion. Some is a bit more subtle: "Craig curled his lip, picked up his gun, and pointed it at her to show he meant business." "Show he meant business" is the author butting in to explain why the character did what he did.

A good rule of thumb is if you can act out what your character is doing, you're showing; if you can't, you're telling. You can't act out "show he meant business."

---

5 Janice Hardy, Understanding Show, Don't Tell: and Really Getting It (Cincinnati, OH: Fiction University Press, 2016).

Told prose can come in both short and long forms. At this stage, the focus shifts from understanding exposition to shaping it at the sentence and paragraph level.

Shorter tells

Shorter tells occur when you tell what a character is feeling, thinking, seeing, hearing, and smelling, or when you tell their motivation.

FIX 1: REMOVE FILTER WORDS

Since filter words affect the narrative distance, I addressed them in full in that topic. But they are also a telling issue. Go to page 143 to read the full explanation with additional examples of filter words.

Example:

> Sergio could **hear** the trumpet, signaling it was time. → The blast from the trumpet woke him up. It was time.

This indicates the sound without stating the character heard it.

FIX 2: USE PHYSICAL ACTION BEATS AND THOUGHTS

To show what a character is feeling, either use physical action beats (averting their gaze to show guilt, darting eye movements to show paranoia) or reveal their thoughts (our emotions come from our thoughts).

Let's say you want to show your character accepting the news that they were fired. You could write something like these examples:

Example 1, using physical actions:

> As his voice droned on, the air seemed to thin. I tugged at my collar and stared at the stain on my pants. Sometime after I'd rubbed

the stain further into my pants, he said, "I have to let you go." I lifted my head, looked him straight in the eye, and nodded.

Example 2, using thoughts:

Just say it already. Geez. I didn't need this. Why was he prolonging it? As the air seemed to thin, I tugged at my collar and stared at the stain on my pants. This couldn't be happening. Not now. How would we get through this? My wife—

"I have to let you go," he said.

Had to? He had to? Bull!

I rubbed my temple. I could do this. "Okay. I understand." I could do this. We would make it. We always did.

FIX 3: USE SENSORY AND OTHER DETAILS

Writers often use the weather to convey a scene's mood, which is now a cliché. You can also show the mood through sensory details.

Make sure to choose sensory and other details that are relevant and convey the mood, the character's perspective, and personality. For example, if your setting is an old, spooky-looking castle, you might show fog, the rustling of leaves, and rotting smells. And don't forget your character's perspective. While it's a scary castle, your character might not be afraid, so you can show their courage and excitement by showing some bright flowers as a contrast or by focusing on some of the castle's more positive aspects: the bright paintings, the expert architecture, etc.

I wrapped my coat around me and ran toward the warmth of the car, the colorful leaves crunching under my feet.

This shows that it's fall and starting to get cold, without telling it.

FIX 4: USE DIALOGUE

The moment you include dialogue, you have an action scene rather than narrative summary. However, if the dialogue's only purpose is to reveal information to the reader and is not something the characters would actually say to each other, then it didn't really fix anything. This is called "As you know, Bob" dialogue and should be avoided.

But if the dialogue exchange is something the characters *would* say, then you have fixed your told prose. For example, instead of telling that Aiden is responsible for his friend's accident and that the friend hasn't forgiven him yet, you can show it through dialogue.

"Honey, you know Aiden feels terrible."

"He should."

"Well, think about his kids. You really want to put them through a lawsuit?"

"Did he think about my kids when he sent off that text? A text! While driving. We aren't dumb teenagers."

Longer tells

In long form, telling can occur over entire paragraphs or an entire scene, essentially summarizing a situation instead of revealing it through action. Not every scene needs to be dramatized; sometimes narrative summary is fine. But when it isn't, those long tells bore the reader. They often come in info dumps, flashbacks, and character backstories. The next topic of this guide discusses info dumps in more depth.

TOLD INFO DUMP

You can fix told info dumps by putting the information in the character's voice and only providing the information the reader needs at that moment.

Info dumps often happen when worldbuilding.

Original:

> Rylan hesitated at the edge of the alley. Leaving the safe zone was dangerous. Ever since the corporate security grid had failed, gangs controlled the streets, and anyone caught alone after dark risked being robbed or worse. Most people stayed inside at night, but Rylan didn't have a choice. He pulled his hood up and stepped into the shadows, hoping no one would notice him.

Revised:

> Rylan's hand found the alley wall. Brick, solid. Better than what waited out there. He pulled his hood up. The fabric rasped against his ears, too loud. But he couldn't back down now. He didn't have a choice. Taking a step forward, he whispered, *I have no choice.* He slid his hands into his jacket, fingers brushing the small knife hidden in the lining. Fat chance that had against the gangs, but it was something. He took another step, the shadows swallowing him whole. Before he could think better of it, he raced into the streets.

In the shown example, the author gives information the reader needs to know at that moment (gangs are out there, and he is only going out because he doesn't have a choice) but doesn't give information the reader doesn't need to know at that moment (security grid had failed). And now the told information is in the character's voice, not the author dumping information.

Info dumping can also occur when a character enters a new setting, and instead of letting the character experience it, the author butts in and explains the setting.

Original:

> Diane entered the old theater on Fifth Street. It had been built in 1923 by the famous architect James Whitmore as a vaudeville house, then converted to a movie palace in the 1940s. Now the Art Deco trim was half-stripped. The city had tried to save it three times over the years, but developers kept blocking the preservation efforts. Now items were up for auction, and it was scheduled for demolition next month to make way for luxury condos. So she had to find the film reels soon.

The information about the theater's history has nothing to do with why Diane is there, and it doesn't sound like thoughts she would naturally think in that moment.

Revised:

> Diane pushed through the theater doors, and the smell hit her: velvet rot and plaster dust. Her grandmother's perfume had smelled like that, toward the end. She ran her hand along the lobby wall where the Art Deco trim was already half-stripped. Some idiot with a crowbar, probably. Selling it online piece by piece before the wrecking balls came.
>
> The auction notice was still taped to the box office window, flapping in the draft. Final Sale. Feb. 10. Two weeks. Just two weeks to find the film reels her dad swore he'd hidden in the projection booth.

Now we get Diane's personal stakes, the ticking clock, her actual mission, and a sense of the theater's fate—all through what matters to her in this moment, not a history lecture.

Info dumps are common enough and complex enough to deserve their own topic (see Craft Effective Exposition on page 175).

TOLD BACKSTORY

Backstory occurs when you pause the forward momentum of the story to explain a character's history or why something is important.
Original:

> [Imagine a scene where a character named Trevin is interviewing a witness to a murder, and in the middle of the dialogue, the author stops the story with this backstory.] He'd just recently become a consultant. Before that, he was a cop. But his partner had it out for him, and he lied under oath, testifying that Trevin had shot a robber without provocation to cover up his involvement in the scheme. He stated that Trevin had switched sides and was actually a loyal member of the crime lord's team, not just an undercover cop pretending to be one. As a result, he was fired and couldn't return to the police force. The FBI hired him as a freelance consultant only after he came to them with all the information they needed to track down a wanted criminal.

First off, this information isn't necessary to know at this very moment. Trevin is currently investigating a murder, so why does the reader need to know his whole backstory in the middle of questioning a witness? Second, the reader will be annoyed that, in the middle of a scene with action (a dialogue questioning a witness), the author butts in and halts the forward action.

If the reader needs the information, integrate it into the action where it matters, and use only short snippets.

Revised:

> Perhaps before Trevin starts questioning the witness, he looks over at his police uniform hanging in his closet and says he doesn't know why he keeps it, since the force will never let him back on after his partner betrayed him. Now the reader knows he used to be a cop. They may be intrigued about what happened, but for now, that's all they need to know.
>
> Then, in a later scene where he's investigating the current crime, he stumbles on evidence proving that his partner was really the one working for the crime lord. He can tell his best friend what he found, thinking this might help him get back on the force.

TOLD FLASHBACK

Authors mistakenly believe a flashback scene is their solution to show, don't tell—particularly when it comes to the backstory. Since it's a scene, not a summary, it's shown, right? Not necessarily. If you're stopping the story's forward action to give a flashback scene, it can still feel like telling, like the author is butting in to give the reader information.

> Let's say you have a scene where Trevin runs into his former partner, and then the author stops the scene to give a flashback to when they were in the courtroom, with his partner testifying against him (showing the betrayal).

Even though it's a scene, it feels like told information.

Revised:

> Instead of stopping the forward action to flash back to the courtroom when his partner betrays him, you can show Trevin's anger

at his partner. Maybe you don't even show why he's angry yet; you just let the reader feel it. Then, in another scene where he encounters his partner, he can say, "So how's your real boss doing these days? You know, Drake [the name of the crime lord]?" Then his partner responds with something like, "You should be thanking your lucky stars Drake doesn't come after you. You could have blown up his entire organization. You were good undercover; I'll give you that."

Or maybe Trevin never runs into his old partner. Instead, maybe he's having a drink in a bar and overhears someone talking about Drake's most recent crime. Trevin could go back to the bar and order a bunch of drinks, mumbling in a drunken stupor about how he was so close to getting Drake off the streets if it weren't for his partner being a dirty cop working for Drake.

In all of these ideas, we get snippets of Trevin's backstory without a long flashback.

Self-editing in practice

Original:

Samantha felt nervous as she walked into the coffee shop. She knew she shouldn't have been late, but the traffic had been terrible, and she hated disappointing her friends. She saw her friend Julia sitting at a corner table and realized Julia looked annoyed. Samantha thought about all the times she had been late in the past and felt guilty again.

Julia had been working at the café for three years and was very protective of her space there. She'd learned to deal with rude customers and disorganized coworkers, but she hated it when friends arrived late. She didn't say anything yet, but Samantha could tell that Julia was irritated by the way she was tapping her fingers on the table and frowning.

Samantha placed her bag on the chair next to her and apologized. She explained that she had had to rush from her apartment across town and traffic was bad. She knew Julia had probably heard this story before. Julia replied that it was fine, but Samantha realized her tone sounded forced and worried she'd ruined the mood.

The coffee shop smelled strongly of burned espresso, and Samantha could hear the whir of the grinders and the chatter of other customers. She noticed that the barista had changed since last time, and she thought about how fast time seemed to pass. Samantha felt anxious because she had her own life to deal with after losing her job, but she'd promised she would be here for Julia this week (generated by ChatGPT).

PAUSE HERE

Open your personalized workbook on your computer and review the practice exercise, asking

- Which sentences express emotions using filter words?

- Which sentences explain a character's motivation instead of showing it?

- Which sensory details are generic instead of filtered through the character?

- What actions or physical beats could replace a told emotion?

- Where could a thought or an interior reaction replace a summary of the character's thoughts?

After answering, revise the scene to show instead of tell, then read my revision.

Revised:

Samantha pushed open the café door, the bell above jingling. Her shoes squeaked against the tile as she scanned the tables. There—Julia sat in the corner, tapping a sharp rhythm on the corner table. Samantha swallowed. Julia wouldn't let her tardiness go. Not this time.

Forcing a smile, she slid into the chair. "Sorry I'm late." Her bag thumped against the floor. "Traffic was insane."

Julia's lips pressed together. "Finally."

Samantha's stomach churned. She dug into her tote for her notebook, jostling pens and papers. The aroma of espresso hit her in waves, mingling with the faint burned sugar smell of the pastries. Machines whirred behind the counter, and laughter bounced off the walls. She hadn't laughed like that since . . . She sucked in a breath. With one hand, she hugged her bag to her chest; with the other, she tapped her fingers on the table, matching Julia's tempo. Mirroring was a way to calm the other person, at least if David's woo-woo talk could be believed.

"Did you hear back from your interview?" Julia asked, eyes flicking toward the street.

"Yeah. They called this morning. Still deciding, I guess. I'm glad I made it here, though . . . I didn't want to miss today."

"Well, you're here now. That's what counts."

Samantha exhaled and let her bag drop fully to the floor.

I rewrote to use various showing-instead-of-telling strategies:

- *Got rid of told emotions and showed them instead through physical action beats and thoughts.*
- *Removed filter words: "felt," "realized," "could tell," "noticed," and "thought."*
- *Got rid of told character motivations: "she hated disappointing her friends" and "she worried she'd ruined the mood."*
- *Deleted Julia's backstory (working at the café) because it wasn't important for this scene.*
- *Changed the told sensory detail—"the coffee shop smelled strongly of burned espresso"—and instead tied it into the character's experience.*

EDITING STEPS

❑ Search for filter words using Word's Find feature and rewrite to get rid of them. (You can also use a macro that will highlight all of them for you. AI is pretty good at creating macros.)

❑ Fix passages that tell emotions; instead, show them either through physical action beats or thoughts.

❑ Cut anything that explains a character's motivation, and show it instead.

❑ Use sensory details to show the character's perspective and scene mood.

❑ Fix longer chunks of told information by
  - deleting what isn't necessary to know in that moment
  - using natural dialogue, not "As you know, Bob" dialogue
  - putting the information in the character's voice and in a way that's natural for them to be thinking at that moment

❑ Integrate characters' backstories into the action throughout or delete if unnecessary.

Craft Effective Exposition (Avoid Info Dumping)

Crafting effective exposition is a big topic, so I just focus on avoiding info dumping, a type of ineffective exposition. Info dumping is when you dump a chunk of information in a reader's lap. This occurs when you're revealing information about your novel's world/society or characters' backstories.

Too much info dumping ruins a reader's experience by stalling the action. It's boring to read and takes the reader out of the experience.

Example:

> Cathy looked down at her dress. It was the best one she could find. Her husband's business had tanked, and she'd sold her fancy dresses in order to pay the bills. Since her friends didn't know, they'd invited her to the annual social fundraiser. She was determined to go. But her husband, Greg, didn't think it was a good idea. She'd met Greg when his business was booming. As he had come from a long line of wealth, she assumed she would never find herself in this position. But here she was. She wasn't going to let Greg's mistakes cloud her social life.

This dumps information without any action, and on top of that, it's information the character wouldn't naturally be thinking about in that moment. The narrator butts in to say that her husband's business had tanked, which is why she's wearing a simple dress rather than a fancy one, that his business was booming previously, and that she'd thought she would never have to struggle financially.

Info dumping in dialogue

In an effort to avoid info dumping, authors put the information in dialogue. But this doesn't solve the problem. Yes, the information is now coming from the characters rather than the narrator, but it's no better than narrative info dumping.

If the only point of the dialogue is to give the reader information, then it isn't natural dialogue. In the editorial world, we refer to this as "As you know, Bob" explanations. This is when the characters share information they already know.

Example:

> Cathy looked down at her dress. It was the best one she could find. Turning to her husband, she said, "I had to sell all my good dresses to pay for the bills since you made that bad business decision. So now this is the only thing I have to wear. I never thought I would see this day. When we had met, your business was booming, and since you came from a long line of wealth, I thought we would never struggle this way."

This is unnatural dialogue that serves only to feed information to the reader. It's still info dumping, just in dialogue form.

Info dumping in flashbacks

Some authors try to fix their info dumping with flashbacks, but just like dialogue, flashbacks can also be a form of info dumping. If you stop the story's forward momentum for a full-on flashback scene, it can annoy readers and take them out of the experience. Readers want to know what will happen next, not what happened in the past.

That being said, flashbacks *can* work if they're firmly woven into the present story and don't take up too much room. When done well, they can create dramatic tension and add texture to a story. To pull this off, keep the flashback brief—a few sentences—and launch right into the forward momentum of the story.

Example:

> "Cathy, I'm looking forward to your presentation this afternoon," her boss said. After returning what she hoped looked like a confident smile, Cathy pressed her hand to her stomach. She walked into her office and rubbed her temples. **She hadn't given a presentation since high school. In biology, in front of everyone, she'd talked to the dead frog. Had full-on talked to a damn dead frog, begging for it to end, and it had . . . when she passed out. She wasn't that girl anymore.** But the kids' taunts increased the pounding in her head. They had—
>
> No, she couldn't go down that route. Using the breathing exercise her therapist had taught her, Cathy stilled her heart as Mark walked by her office. She ran out to flag him down. "Mark, do you think I could run my presentation by you one more time?"

The bolded part is a brief flashback, but it's short and tightly woven into the scene.

How to fix info dumping

Start by cutting anything the reader doesn't need to know at all. With what remains, ask whether they need it *now*. If not, save it for later. If it's necessary information and only a couple of sentences remain, keep it as is. Anything more should be fixed using one of the two methods below.

The first is turning it into a shown info dump, where the information is filtered through the character's voice and perspective. If you haven't read the "Master Show and Tell" lesson, read just the info dump section (starts on page 166) before continuing.

The second is turning the info dump into a scene, either by building a scene around the information or weaving it into an existing one.

Original:

> Let's say the reader needs to know that Cathy was bullied as a child. Originally, the author included a four-paragraph info dump explaining that she was bullied, why she was bullied, how they bullied her, and the lasting effects.
>
> But the reader doesn't need to know how Cathy was bullied at all. They need to know why, but not in this scene—that can come later. And while they need to understand the effects, those can be shown throughout the story rather than explained up front.
>
> So the author deletes everything except the basic fact: Cathy was bullied as a child. But even that information shouldn't be conveyed as exposition.

Revised 1: Weave it into an existing scene

> If the next scene shows another character being picked on, have Cathy react immediately, coming to their defense, acting protective, and making a comment that reveals her past. "I know what that feels like" says everything without explaining anything. The why and how the bullying affected her will then emerge naturally through the story at a later point.

Revised 2: Build a new scene

If the surrounding scenes don't provide an opportunity, create one. Maybe a coworker makes a snide remark to Cathy. She snaps back harder than expected: "I dealt with enough bullies growing up. I'm not putting up with it now." That single moment of reaction tells the reader what they need to know.

The idea is to remove what isn't necessary to know in the moment (that scene, that chapter, that plot point) and try to turn what is needed into a scene or short shown info dump. If you can't turn it into a scene or a showing version, reduce the info dump to just a few sentences.

Self-editing in practice

Original:

Lena sat at the kitchen table, staring at the envelope in her hands. It was from the University of Chicago, where her father had gone before he dropped out during the protests in the 1970s. After leaving school, he'd wandered for years before meeting her mother in New Mexico, where they started their family in a commune. Growing up there had taught Lena how to live simply, without running water or electricity, though she'd hated it at the time. She'd sworn she'd never live that way again. Now, with this letter in her hand, she wondered if her past was about to catch up with her.

Her brother walked in.

"You're holding that envelope awfully tight," he said. "Remember how Dad always regretted leaving school, especially after the protest that got him arrested? He always wanted one of us to go back to Chicago and make it right. Mom was furious when she found out about his arrest, but she still stood by him because she loved him. That's why this is such a big deal."

Lena's mind drifted back. She was six years old, sitting cross-legged on the dirt floor of their commune's main hut while her parents argued in hushed voices about leaving. She had hated the way her hair smelled like smoke every night, hated the thin blankets, hated the endless lentils. She remembered crying herself to sleep, whispering to herself that one day she'd escape.

The letter crinkled in her hands as she shook her head (generated by ChatGPT).

PAUSE HERE

Open your personalized workbook on your computer and review the practice exercise, asking

- Which sentences pause the story to explain character history or worldbuilding?
- What information would the POV character naturally think about in this moment?
- What information is only there to help the reader, not the character?
- Which details are unnecessary right now and could be woven in later?

After answering, revise the scene to avoid info dumping, then read my revision.

Problems with original:

This scene has all three kinds of info dumps: narrative info dump (paragraph about her father's history and her backstory), dialogue info dump (brother reminding Lena of things she already knows), and flashback info dump (full childhood memory).

Revised:

> Lena sat at the kitchen table, staring at the envelope in her hands. The University of Chicago seal glared up at her like a dare. Her chest tightened. So much for never letting her past follow her into her future. Her past was here, pressing into her palm.
>
> Her brother walked in and leaned against the doorframe. "You're squeezing that thing like it might bite."
>
> "Maybe it will."
>
> He crossed the room and pulled out a chair. "Dad always wished he'd stayed. Guess now it's your turn to decide."
>
> Lena's throat tightened at the mention of their father. She didn't need a history lesson—she remembered all too well. His regrets had been thick in the air of their house, as constant as the smell of wood smoke from their commune days. And those hushed arguments? The walls were too thin, and her pillow did nothing to help her escape. More nights than she could count, she'd fallen asleep swearing she'd escape that life. Now the letter trembled between her fingers, as if daring her to prove she had.

I removed all the info dumps and wove the information into the action.

EDITING STEPS

❑ Look for areas where you tell chunks of information without anything happening in the moment.

❑ Determine whether each of those areas is okay as is:
- If it's brief, it's probably fine. You do need to tell some information.
- If it's longer but stays in the character's voice, it's a shown info dump and is likely fine.

❑ Determine whether the reader must know that information in that moment. If they don't, delete that information from that scene and integrate it later when it's important to know.

❑ For any info dump that's necessary in the moment, fix it by
- building a scene around it (just make sure you don't include any "As you know, Bob" dialogue)
- building the information into an already existing scene
- changing it to a shown info dump

Delete Unnecessary Explanations

While some small explanations may be okay here and there, too much explaining intrudes on the story and the readers' experience. Explanations can cause readers to feel

- cheated that they weren't allowed to piece things together themselves
- annoyed, like "Okay. I get it"
- insulted that the author felt the need to spell it out

Most of the time, if you have to explain something for readers to understand the story, you need to rework your scene or your characters. In other words, you shouldn't *need* to explain. Either trust that your readers will get it or realize that you need to more fully develop the scene, the characters, or both.

Telling what you just showed or what was already implied

While sometimes you need to tell and other times you can show, you should never both tell *and* show the same information. Let the "showing" speak for itself.

Unnecessary explanations commonly occur when authors explain what the dialogue just said.

Example:

> "I'm sorry, Carol, we have to let you go."
>
> "Uh . . . what? Um . . . okay. Do I get paid for this week and some sort of severance pay? How could you do this? I thought we were friends."
>
> Carlos rubbed his face and, without looking her in the eyes, said, "Yes, you'll get this week's pay. I'm not authorized to offer severance. This is completely out of my hands."
>
> Carol picked up her things without looking at her boss, who was also her friend. She couldn't believe Carlos would do this to her. At least she got her pay, but no severance. No severance. That was crazy! Who do they think they are?

The dialogue already showed us that she and Carlos were friends, that she couldn't believe Carlos would fire her, and that she got her pay but no severance. The internal dialogue is fine (presented in free indirect speech), but the narration after the interiority merely explains what the dialogue already said.

Unnecessary explanation also occurs in narration. You don't need to explain what can easily be implied or what was already made clear from the text.

Examples:

> She got too close to her and stepped on her sandals.

Stepping on her sandals in and of itself implies that she got too close to her, so we don't need that detail.

He'd saved up for months to buy Ned the action figure, the newest toy craze. All the kids wanted one.

The "newest toy craze" already suggests that all the kids want one, so delete the last sentence.

Sighing, she bent down and tried to repair the shoes. As she attempted to figure out a way to tie the torn straps together, a man stumbled over her.

The text already stated that she tried to repair the shoes, so there's no need to repeat it in the next sentence.

Brinley's hand shot into the air. The teacher looked at her hand, sighed, and looked around at the other students. After a moment, he repeated the question, looking around again. Brinley always answered the questions, so he wanted to give other students a chance.

The first three sentences show that Brinley always answers the questions. No need to then tell us after you found a way to show it.

Explaining characters' behavior

It should be clear from the events, the dialogue, and the characters' personalities and desires why a character did what they did. You can usually spot this mistake—explaining a character's behavior—by looking for certain words: because, so that, in order to, like, as if, and since, etc.

Examples:

> This appeared in a scene right after the character's friend told him his wife had lied to him and wasn't home: He called his wife to find out if it was true.

The reason for calling is clear.

> The scene just said someone knocked, and then we have: She saw him glance at the door. He must have heard the knock interrupting their fight, just as she had.

The reader knows why he glanced at the door.

> Wanting to ensure her husband knew where she'd gone, she left him a note telling him where she was and when she would be back.

Why else would she leave him that note?

> He wiped the gun down before burying it so that his fingerprints wouldn't be on the gun.

Pretty sure the reader can infer that was the reason for wiping down the gun.

Beating a dead horse

This one isn't necessarily an explanation, but it's related. Even if you show instead of tell, you don't need to repeat the same details over and over. Whether repetition appears in dialogue, as showing narration, or as telling narration, if a point has been made very clearly, it can annoy readers if you keep repeating it.

Example:

> Let's say it's essential to know a character was abused as a kid and feels anger from it since that sets up his motivations. If he reflects on his past with anger every single time he hears someone raise their voice, or sees a kid cry, or witnesses abuse, the reader may feel annoyed. This isn't to say you couldn't show the character reflecting on his past more than once. After all, we reflect on the same past incident many times. You just don't want to overdo it.

Self-editing in practice

Original:

> Daniella sat across from Lance at the coffee shop. "I think we should break up."
>
> "What? After two years?" Lance leaned back in his chair. He couldn't believe what he was hearing.
>
> "I'm sorry."
>
> Lance stood up and nearly knocked over his chair. "I need to go," he muttered. He grabbed his jacket from the back of his chair so that he could leave the coffee shop.
>
> Daniella reached out to touch his arm in an attempt to make him stay. He pulled away without looking at her and walked out.
>
> Daniella watched him through the window. This reminded her of when her mother left her father. Her father had cried for weeks. Now she was doing the same thing her mother had done—hurting someone who loved her.

The barista approached her table. "Miss, are you okay?"

Daniella wiped her eyes. "I'm fine."

She looked at Lance's half-finished coffee still sitting on the table. It was still there because he had left so quickly. Daniella stood up but was too close to the table and bumped it. She grabbed her side and winced (generated by Claude because ChatGPT's output was bad, no matter how I tried to prompt it).

> ## PAUSE HERE
>
> Open your personalized workbook on your computer and review the practice exercise, asking
>
> - Does the narration repeat what the dialogue already showed? If so, where?
> - Does the narration explain motivations the reader can already infer?
> - What can you delete without losing clarity?
>
> After answering, revise the passage to remove unnecessary explanations, then read my revision.

Problem with original:

This passage repeats information the dialogue already showed and explains what the reader can infer.

Revised:

Daniella sat across from Lance at the coffee shop. "I think we should break up."

"What? After two years?" Lance leaned back in his chair.

"I'm sorry."

Lance stood up and nearly knocked over his chair. "I need to go," he muttered. He grabbed his jacket from the back of his chair.

Daniella reached out to touch his arm. He pulled away without looking at her and walked out.

Daniella watched him through the window. It was her mother and father all over again. Her father had cried for weeks. Now she was doing the same thing her mother had done.

The barista approached her table. "Miss, are you okay?"

Daniella wiped her eyes. "I'm fine."

She looked at Lance's half-finished coffee still sitting on the table. Daniella stood up and bumped into the table. She grabbed her side and winced.

I deleted the unnecessary explanations:

- *He couldn't believe what he was hearing*
- *So that he could leave the coffee shop*
- *In an attempt to make him stay*
- *Because he'd left so quickly*
- *But was too close to the table*

EDITING STEPS

- ❏ Search for explanation trigger words like "because," "so that," "in order to," "since," etc. Then delete the explanation if it's already clear from context.
- ❏ Read your dialogue and the narration that follows. If the narration repeats what the dialogue already reveals, delete it.
- ❏ Track repeated information (the same backstory, motivation, or detail). Keep the strongest instance (or instances, if a character would naturally reflect on it more than once) and delete the rest.
- ❏ Check any exposition after a showing moment and delete anything that repeats what the showing already revealed.

Strengthen Dialogue

Dialogue for dialogue's sake never works. It should always reveal information about a character or move the action along.

If your dialogue meets that criterion, then keep it. But make sure it's natural and shows your character's unique voice.

Unnatural dialogue

Unnatural dialogue can come in many forms, including characters

- saying something they wouldn't naturally say
- being overly formal and perfectly grammatical
- never being interrupted and always being perfectly understood

Dialogue doesn't work if a character wouldn't actually say those words. In the "Master Show and Tell" and "Craft Effective Exposition" topics, I mentioned "As you know, Bob" dialogue. This is when your characters are saying things everyone in the scene knows; the only purpose is to catch the reader up to speed. You want to avoid that.

> "Well, remember, in our society, those with great skills and talents are told to limit themselves so they don't make us too jealous," said Kelly.
>
> Erin replied, "Yeah. I'm glad I'm one of the talentless so I don't have to try too hard to fit in. I do need to meet with the Council,

the ones in charge of keeping us the same, every week to ensure that I remain one of the talentless."

This isn't natural because the characters already know this information. It's also too stiff and formal.

Sometimes dialogue isn't "As you know, Bob," but it still isn't natural for that character to say in that moment. When writing dialogue, consider the character's motivations and desires, as those two things impact what they say, how they say it, and when they say it.

Let's say Nina is a sharp, ambitious junior associate at a law firm. She's been working late nights, desperate to prove herself to the partners. She finally gets a rare chance to present in a big meeting. She's terrified of seeming inexperienced in front of the senior lawyers—her whole desire in this moment is to *project confidence,* and she says, "Well, honestly, I'm still kind of figuring this out, but maybe we could . . ."

That's perfectly natural dialogue. Lots of people hedge when they're unsure. But it doesn't seem realistic for Nina to say this, as it's directly contrary to her goal of appearing confident.

Another trademark of unnatural dialogue is being overly formal. Unless it's distinct to their character, it's unlikely that characters will use formal language, complete sentences, and perfect grammar in all their exchanges.

"She has fewer grapes than I."

While technically grammatically "correct," most people would say, "She has less grapes than me," and that's okay.

So feel free to break some grammar rules, and while you're at it, sprinkle in some natural fragments.

No fragments	Responding in fragments
"Are you okay?" "No, I'm not okay."	"Are you okay?" "Nope. Not okay."
"Did the teacher really say that?" "It doesn't matter if she did or didn't. She's moving, so she can't teach next year anyway."	"Did the teacher really say that?" "Doesn't matter. She's moving, so can't teach next year anyway."

The last type of unnatural dialogue occurs when you don't have any interruptions or misunderstandings. In real life, people interrupt each other, misunderstand each other, or respond vaguely. So if your characters never do either, your dialogue may be lacking.

> "What on earth did you think you were doing, Jill?" Jack said. "You could have burned the bloody house down. I don't get—"
>
> "I'm okay, really . . ."

In this dialogue exchange, Jill interrupted Jack, and she didn't actually answer his question, because she's preoccupied with something.

Of course, if interruptions and misunderstandings happen too much, that's also a problem. The truth is, dialogue in a book won't be a 100 percent like real conversations. We don't want our characters to stop mid-sentence, repeat themselves, interrupt, hesitate, stutter, use filler words, have mundane conversations, etc. as often as we do in real life. The dialogue needs to sound realistic but not so lifelike that it gets bogged down.

Unique character voice

If every character sounds the same, you have a dialogue problem even if it's all natural.

To vary the dialogue, think of the following for each character:

- Does the character use any habitual phrases?
- How polite or impolite is the character?
- Is the character shy or more outgoing? Wordy or more succinct? Awkward or confident?
- Are there certain words the character would never use (vile words, complicated words, obscure words, etc.)? Are there obscure words they would use?

Take a look at a dialogue exchange between two characters:

"It's 6:12. The shuttle leaves at 6:15. If we're not there, we miss it. Period," Jordan said.

Sam said, "Time is a construct, my friend. The shuttle doesn't *really* leave until the driver decides to step on the gas."

"Yeah. Which will be at 6:15. Exactly."

"Fine, fine. I think if destiny wanted us on that bus, destiny would also want me to have a snack first. You know, fuel for fate."

"Destiny's going to leave you behind eating chips. And I'm not covering for you again if we're late. Professor Klein already thinks you're unreliable."

"Unreliable? I'm the very picture of dependability. I just operate on a . . . looser interpretation of deadlines."

"You mean you ignore them."

"Semantics. Tomato, tomahto" (generated by ChatGPT).

Jordan's voice is more succinct. He avoids fluff and speaks in concrete terms. He isn't rude; he's just not indulgent with his words. Sam, on the other hand, is more wordy, playful, and sarcastic. She's prone to exaggeration and whimsical phrases.

Self-editing in practice

Original A:

Revise for natural dialogue.

"That was the longest day of my life," Shawn said, flipping the sign to CLOSED.

"Yeah, but at least the event went well," Lena said. "The author even said she wants to come back in December for the holiday crowd."

"Good. That makes Sarah happy. She's been trying to increase in-store events since the winter fundraiser last year."

Lena nodded. "Right. Because in-store events are what drive the most foot traffic in quarter four," she said.

Shawn glanced at her. "Did you talk to her about next Saturday?"

"Not yet." She straightened a stack of gift bags that didn't need straightening. "I figured I could email her Monday with the formal request and explain the context."

"I thought you said your sister's rehearsal dinner is Friday night. You kinda need the whole weekend."

"I do. It's just . . . Sarah seemed stressed today. And I didn't want to add to it by bringing up my personal obligations when she was already talking about staffing gaps and how Saturdays are critical for revenue."

"Lena, she knows your sister is getting married. You told her like a month ago when we were doing the floor reset."

"Yes, but at that time I merely mentioned it in passing. I didn't formally ask for the day off."

"You don't have to be formal," Shawn said, laughing. "Just tell her you can't work."

"I don't want to seem unreliable. They just promoted me to key-holder, and if I immediately start declining weekend shifts, it reflects poorly on my commitment to the store."

"You literally cover for everyone. She's not gonna think you're unreliable."

"I know. I'm still kind of figuring things out, and maybe the wedding isn't actually that big of a deal" (generated by ChatGPT).

PAUSE HERE

Open your personalized workbook on your computer and review the practice exercise, asking

- What lines feel unrealistic for the character in this moment?

- Is any line "As you know, Bob" dialogue?

- Does the conversation ever feel too formal, polished, or stiff?

- What could make the dialogue feel more realistic?

After answering, revise the dialogue to make it more natural before reading my revision.

Problems with original:

This scene contains "as you know, Bob" dialogue, some of it's too formal and polished, one line isn't true to what the character would say, and nobody interrupts or misunderstands (you don't necessarily need this last one, but I'm throwing it in here for practicing purposes).

Revised A:

> "That was the longest day of my life," Shawn said, flipping the sign to CLOSED.
>
> "Yeah, but at least the event went well," Lena said. "The author even said she wants to come back in December for the holiday crowd."
>
> "Good. Sarah will be happy," Shawn said, then glanced at her. "Did you talk to her about next Saturday?"
>
> "Not yet." She straightened a stack of gift bags that didn't need straightening. "I can email her and explain the context."
>
> "I thought you said your sister's rehearsal dinner is Friday night. You kinda need the whole weekend."
>
> "I do. It's just . . . Sarah seemed stressed today. I didn't want to add to it by bringing it up when she was already talking about staffing gaps and—"
>
> "Lena, she knows your sister is getting married. You told her like a month ago when we were doing the floor reset."
>
> "Yes, but only in passing. I didn't formally ask for the day off."
>
> "You don't have to be formal," Shawn said, laughing. "Just tell her you can't work."
>
> "I don't want to seem unreliable. They just promoted me to keyholder, so requesting weekends off isn't really a good look."

"You literally cover for everyone. She's not gonna think you're unreliable."

"I know. I'm still kind of figuring things out. I have to attend that wedding. It's just . . . I don't know."

Deleted the "as you know, Bob" dialogue (the part about Lena trying to increase the store events) and changed dialogue that sounded too formal. To make the dialogue even more natural, I added an interruption and removed the dialogue that wasn't true to character (Lena saying the wedding isn't a big deal).

Original B:

Revise for unique character voice.

Aria slammed her textbook shut. "I can't believe Professor Chen is making our final exam cumulative. We have to know everything from the entire semester."

"Well, you know how Professor Chen always makes his exams really hard because he wants to weed out the students who aren't serious about pre-med," Derek said.

Casey looked up from her laptop. "At least you guys have finals. My marketing professor just assigned a group project instead."

"Lucky you," Aria said. "I have been studying for this exam for three weeks straight. I cannot afford to receive anything less than an A."

Derek stretched out on his bed. "You're going to do fine. You always do fine."

"That's easy for you to say. Your philosophy exam is probably just going to ask you to write an essay about Plato or something."

"Actually, it's on Kant's *Categorical Imperative* and its applications to modern ethical dilemmas," Derek said.

Casey closed her laptop. "You know, Aria, stress isn't good for memory retention. Studies show that high cortisol levels can actually impair your ability to recall information during exams."

"I know you're trying to help, but I cannot simply turn off my anxiety," Aria said.

Derek sat up. "Maybe you should try some meditation or something."

"Meditation isn't going to help me remember the Krebs cycle," Aria said.

Casey packed her things. "Well, I'm going to go study in the library where it's quieter."

"That sounds like a good idea. I should probably do the same thing," Derek said.

Aria gathered her books. "Yes, I think we should all go to the library. It'll be more conducive to studying than this room."

"Great, so we're all in agreement then," Casey said (generated by ChatGPT).

PAUSE HERE

- What habitual phrases, tones, or quirks could emerge?

- What vocabulary, humor, formality, or sentence length could differ for each character?

- Would each character actually speak like this, given their personalities and desires?

After answering, revise to ensure a unique and natural character voice, then read my revision.

Revised B:

Aria slammed her textbook shut. "I can't believe Professor Chen is making our final exam cumulative."

"Ugh. Chen's the worst. But you know 'it'll separate the wheat from the chaff.'" Derek stuck his nose in the air and posed like the professor.

Casey looked up from her laptop. "At least you guys *have* finals. My marketing professor just assigned a group project instead."

"Lucky you," Aria said. "I have been studying for this thing for three weeks straight, so much information that I knew before, but now. Gah, I'm still gonna—"

"You'll be fine. You always freak out and then ace everything." Derek stretched out on his bed.

"That's easy for you to say. Your philosophy exam is probably just gonna be, like, write an essay about Plato or whatever."

"Actually, it's on Kant's *Categorical Imperative,*" Derek said.

Casey closed her laptop. "Aria, breathe. Stress hurts memory retention. And my head."

"I can't just turn off my anxiety. That's not how—"

"Meditate or something. Geez. Chill." Derek sat up.

"Meditation? Seriously? Meditation's going to help me remember the Krebs cycle?"

"I mean . . . maybe?" Derek picked up his phone.

Casey packed her things. "Well, I'm going to the library. It's too chaotic here."

"Good idea. Wanna come, Aria?" Derek said.

Aria gathered her books. "I'm going to fail. You're all bailing. Everyone in the library is just gonna, like, be all calm and studious, rubbing my nose in it." She sighed. "Yeah . . . okay. Maybe a change of scenery will help."

"Or make you more anxious," Casey muttered under her breath.

Everyone now has a distinct voice. Aria is anxious and rambling; Derek is laid-back and gives simple responses; Casey is direct, practical, and slightly sarcastic. We also have some interruptions, and I added less formal grammar ("gonna," "wanna," contractions, shorter sentences for natural responses, etc.).

EDITING STEPS

❑ Make sure all your dialogue either reveals character or advances the plot.

❑ Make sure your dialogue is natural by eliminating dialogue that contains

- characters telling each other things they already know (as you know, Bob)
- overly formal, always perfectly grammatical language
- content unnatural for the character to say in that moment (unrelated to their motivations and desires)
- dialogue exchanges that are always too perfect, where everyone always understands each other and lets each other finish their sentences (But be careful not to overdo this. We do want your dialogue to be more "perfect" than in real life to keep the forward momentum.)

❑ Check that a character's dialogue is unique to how the character would talk:

- Speech patterns
- Vocabulary
- Tone

Refine Tags and Beats

Dialogue tags identify who's speaking (e.g., "she said," "he whispered") and sometimes include how they're talking. Action beats are actions a character performs during a dialogue exchange—before, during, or after they speak (e.g., She slammed the door. "I'm done.").

Overusing either—or using them poorly—can weaken your dialogue.

Dialogue tags

You may have solid dialogue, but common dialogue tag pitfalls can weaken it.

PITFALL 1: OVERTAGGING

You don't need to tag every line of dialogue. Only tag when

- We need to know who said it
- The character took a specific, need-to-know action while talking at the same time
- We learn information about the character from the tag

In the last two situations, you could also use an action beat rather than a tag.

PITFALL 2: USING "CREATIVE" TAGS (OR UNNECESSARY ONES)

Some editors and authors say you should never use tags other than the standard "said," "whispered," "yelled." Others say to use different tags for variety.

In this instance, variety isn't a good thing. Standard tag words are invisible to the reader, while creative tags call attention to the fact that a story is being told and could pull readers out of that story. If you have one or two creative tags used with intention, fine. But for the most part, I suggest sticking to the standard ones.

And definitely don't use unnecessary tags that describe what is already clear: "replied," "interrupted," etc. If someone spoke before the character and that character is now speaking, it's clear they're replying. If the previous character doesn't finish what they're saying, then it's clear this character is interrupting them.

PITFALL 3: USING ADVERBS

Most of the time, you should remove adverbs from your dialogue tags.

Could you imagine going to see a play and after certain lines of dialogue, the author stands up and says, "Okay, so just now the character said that angrily," or "the character said that annoyingly"? It would take you out of the experience. The same thing happens when you're reading.

Of course, you don't have someone on stage acting out the emotion, so you need to show it through words. But that is doable without using an adverb.

PITFALL 4: NOT VARYING THE TAGS

Variety is the spice of life (except when it comes to actual tag words, as I just discussed). You can vary your tags through placement and tag level.

Placement: You can place your tags at the beginning, in the middle, or at the end. Mixing up where you put the tags when you have to have several in a row will help smooth out the dialogue.

Level: There are three levels of tags.

- Level 1: Hassan said (who said it)
- Level 2: Hassan mumbled (who + how said it)
- Level 3: Hassan said, looking down at his feet (who + action)

When we need to know who said something, then a level 1 tag works. If it's clear who said it, you shouldn't use a level 1 tag. Throughout your story, use level 2 and level 3 tags as needed to reveal the character and move the action along. You can also just ditch the tag entirely and use action beats instead of a level 2 or 3 tag.

EXAMPLE

This example is a narrative I wrote in college, which I then modified to include all the tag pitfalls I've discussed. Since this narrative is a true account of an incident that happened while I was volunteering in Ecuador, it's not a fictional example; however, it includes dialogue, so it works for our purposes.

Original:

> Jorge said he wanted to talk, to explain, and being who I am, I let him.
>
> "I didn't know it was whiskey; I thought it was water," he said.
>
> "Then why did you just tell Lindsay it was whiskey?" I asked incredulously.
>
> "Because I realized it was whiskey," he confessed.
>
> "So when you went to the bar, you ordered water?" I asked.

"Yes, I got you water," he said.

"But it was alcohol," I exclaimed vehemently.

"Yes," he replied.

"Did you order alcohol or water?" I asked.

"I ordered alcohol, but it was for me, not for you," he insisted.

Two people are talking back and forth, so it's clear who's speaking, yet each line still has a tag. Every tag was a level 1 and came at the end of the line of dialogue. Two used an adverb ("vehemently" and "incredulously"). One used an unnecessary "replied," and two used creative tags ("confessed" and "insisted").

Revised:

Jorge said he wanted to talk, to explain, and being who I am, I let him.

"I didn't know it was whiskey; I thought it was water."

"You can't be serious. Then why did you just tell Lindsay it was whiskey?"

"Because I realized it was whiskey."

"Oh, so when you went to the bar, you actually ordered me water?" I said, letting the sarcasm seep into my voice.

"Yes, I got you water."

"But it was . . . alcohol," I shouted.

He nodded. I looked at Lindsay to assure myself this was real. She just shuffled her feet and shrugged. I was on my own, but at least she too recognized the madness. With the music from the club echoing my beating heart, I took a deep breath. Then emphasizing each word, I asked, "Okay . . . did you order alcohol or water?"

"I ordered alcohol, but it was for me, not for you."

I reduced the number of tags and added "you can't be serious," so the dialogue itself shows the emotion rather than telling it through the use of "incredulously." I moved one tag to the front and removed unnecessary and creative tags. I also switched some tags to action beats.

Action beats

Put simply, an action beat is when a character does an action during a dialogue exchange. These can come before, during, or after a dialogue exchange.

Example of an action beat:

"I know. I'll . . ." Kayla ran her hand through her hair.

PURPOSE OF ACTION BEATS

Sometimes you need your characters to engage in a longer dialogue exchange, but long blocks of dialogue can seem daunting and create a monotonous rhythm. Action beats can help break that up.

My favorite use of action beats is to control rhythm and tension. You can either build or reduce it depending on the number of action beats you use.

- To ramp up the tension, limit the beats or remove them altogether during high-tension dialogue.
- To relax the tension, add more beats. This creates more pauses in the dialogue.

While fewer beats breaking up long dialogue generally raises the tension, you can also insert a longer beat to slow down the scene at a critical moment, thus creating more tension by delaying the big reveal.

Action beats can also help establish setting, as certain beats ground the reader into the scene. For example, if your characters are having a conversation at the beach, you could include an action beat like this:

> Greta curled and uncurled her toes in the sand as the sand pebbles flicked around. "Yeah, I'm not saying you're wrong. I just think we need to slow down."

And lastly, action beats help convey characters' emotions, motivations, and movements. Emotions are expressed in several ways: the words we say, the way we use our bodies, and the tone we use. If the words themselves don't convey the character's emotion, and the reader needs to know that emotion, an action beat can help.

Let's take, for example, the phrase "I don't care." This could be expressed sadly, nonchalantly, or angrily. The words themselves don't tell us how the character is feeling.

> "I don't care." Gary felt a lump growing in his throat and bit his lip, staring at her with a dead expression.

This action beat shows the character holding back his tears.

You can also show a character's emotions through an action beat if their feelings don't match up with their words.

> "Yeah. I trust you. Of course, I trust you. We're in this together." Rodrigo shifted his weight and rubbed his hands on his pants.

This action beat shows us he's nervous despite his confident words.

Action beats can also indicate a character's movement without revealing emotion or motivation.

Robert shut the door and set down his briefcase. "Honey, I'm home."

PITFALL 1: POORLY BALANCED ACTION BEATS

As with all techniques, you don't want to overdo it or create an obvious pattern. If you consistently have three lines of dialogue, then an action beat, then three lines of dialogue, etc., it'll become apparent. And when readers can spot a pattern, they focus on your writing rather than on the story itself.

As mentioned, action beats allow you to vary the pace and rhythm of the dialogue, so you need to think about what the dialogue actually needs when deciding where and how many beats to use. One beat could be too many if it drags down what should be a high-tension scene. But if a given scene doesn't dictate a certain amount of tension, then just ensure it has a good balance of beats, dialogue tags, and actual dialogue. You don't want dialogue to go on and on without any interruption in the form of beats, but you also don't want to turn every dialogue tag into a beat.

Original:

> "I can't believe you found this place," Lilliana said.
>
> Ravi replied, "I know, right? Tucked away in the middle of nowhere, but their pie is supposed to be amazing."
>
> "You and your obsession with pie."
>
> "Hey, if you're going to have a food obsession, there are worse things."
>
> "I guess. So, what's good here?"
>
> "Everything, supposedly. But I heard the blueberry crumble is life-changing."
>
> "Life-changing? That's a big claim."

"Just wait. You'll see."

"Fine, but if it's not the best pie I have ever had, you owe me."

"Deal."

This isn't a high-tension scene, so it could use some action beats to break up the dialogue.

Revised:

"I can't believe you found this place," Lilliana said.

"I know, right? Tucked away in the middle of nowhere, but their pie is supposed to be amazing." **Ravi slid into the booth, already scanning the menu.**

"You and your obsession with pie."

"Hey, if you're going to have a food obsession, there are worse things."

"I guess." **Lilliana picked up her napkin, twisting it between her fingers.** "So, what's good here?"

"Everything, supposedly. But I heard the blueberry crumble is life-changing."

"Life-changing? That's a big claim."

"Just wait. You'll see."

"Fine, but if it's not the best pie I have ever had, you owe me."

Ravi extended his hand. "Deal."

I added in a few action beats but made sure each one had a purpose. They're naturally sprinkled in instead of following a set pattern.

PITFALL 2: RUNNING COMMENTARY ON THE DIALOGUE

Be wary of beats that do little other than comment on what the dialogue already shows. If the dialogue already indicates a character's emotion, you don't need to show it in a beat. You can let your readers imagine how the character expresses the emotion.

Example:

> "Go away . . ." She trailed off and waved her out.

> *The ellipses indicate trailing off, and the words "go away" indicate she wants her out, so this beat isn't serving any purpose.*

PITFALL 3: UNNECESSARILY STATING MOVEMENT

Readers don't need to be told every action; we can connect the dots. If a character is talking on the phone, we know they picked up the phone. No need to say it.

Example:

> The phone rang, disrupting the quiet night. Bobbie Joe walked over to the phone on the wall and picked up the receiver. "Yes, what?"

> *You don't have to add the movement beat. You can just say, "The phone rang, disrupting the quiet night." "Yes, what?"*

Indicating movement is fine, but make sure it serves one of the purposes I discussed previously. For example, it might not be necessary to the plot line to know that a character dropped their fork. But that action beat could establish the scene of sitting at a dinner table, provide tension by prolonging the great reveal, or reduce tension by allowing more pauses and breaks between the dialogue.

But if it isn't serving a purpose other than stating movement, reassess whether the reader could already easily infer a character's movements. Don't write stage directions.

PITFALL 4: UNNECESSARILY NAMING BODY PARTS

Your action beat doesn't need to say "he nodded his head," or "she shrugged her shoulders." What else does one nod and shrug? Watch out for where you might be unnecessarily naming the body parts doing the action.

PITFALL 5: USING TOO MANY CRUTCHES

Be careful not to have your characters always perform the same actions to indicate the same emotions. If your characters always frown or get teary-eyed, think of another way to express sadness. If your characters always smile or chuckle, think of another way to express amusement.

While frowning, nodding, sighing, smiling, rolling eyes, and shrugging tend to be the most common crutch actions, you may have your own crutch action beats. So also look out for ones you use too often. You can run a macro to find these.

Tool

Paul Beverly has a CatchPhrase macro available.[6] It'll count any phrases used over a certain number of times. He also has a CountPhrase macro that'll count the number of times you use a specific phrase.

ProWritingAid has a cliché finder, and you can also ask AI to flag clichés for you. (Make sure to change your settings so it doesn't use your manuscript to train the AI model and your work remains private.)

---

6   Ariele Winters, "How to Use Catch Phrase: A Macro for Fiction Writers," Winters Editing (blog), October 27, 2023, https://wintersediting.com/catch-phrase-macro/.

EXAMPLE

Original:

> "I can't believe you did that," Emma said.
>
> Mateo said, "I didn't have a choice."
>
> "You always say that."
>
> "Well, it's true this time."
>
> "Unbelievable." She sighed.
>
> "Look, I don't need you to understand. I need you to trust me."
>
> She stared at him and said, "And what if I can't?"
>
> Mateo sighed. "Then I guess we're done here."
>
> Emma's fingers curled into a fist. "Just like that?"
>
> He pushed a hand through his hair, his shoulders sagging. "What else do you want me to say?"
>
> She whirled to face him. She wanted the truth. "I want the truth, Mateo. The real truth."

This is a high-tension scene, so we have too many action beats. This also has two uses of the crutch "sighed," an unnecessary naming of a body part, and an action beat with running commentary ("she wanted the truth").

Revised:

> Emma clutched her coffee cup, staring at the rain streaking the window. "I can't believe you did that."
>
> Mateo said, "I didn't have a choice."

"You always say that."

"Well, it's true this time."

"Unbelievable."

"Look, I don't need you to understand. I just need you to trust me."

Emma stared at him, searching for any flicker of guilt, but Mateo's expression remained unreadable. The hum of the refrigerator filled the silence between them, a stark contrast to the storm raging in her chest. She wanted to believe him, wanted to think he hadn't just shattered everything they'd built, but the weight in her stomach told her otherwise. "And what if I can't?"

"Then I guess we're done here."

"Just like that?"

"What else do you want me to say?"

I added in an action beat at the start to establish the character's mood, then I inserted one long action beat to slow the scene down right before the high tension. After that moment, I deleted the rest of the action beats and won't use any more action beats for the remainder of the dialogue until the last line.

If you keep the rest of the action beats, revise them for the other pitfalls.

- Mateo sighed → Mateo let out a slow breath (to avoid the crutch).
- His shoulders sagging → he sagged.
- Before shaking his head → keep, because you can shake other things besides your head.
- She wanted the truth → delete for sure, as this is running commentary on the text.

Self-editing in practice

Original:

"So . . . small thing," Liam said, hesitantly. "Evan's coming Friday."

Jenna looked up from the leftovers she was packing. "This Friday?" she asked.

"Yeah," Liam said quickly. "He got the interview downtown and didn't want to pay for a hotel."

"Liam, I told you I wanted this weekend for the podcast stuff," Jenna said, trying to keep her voice even.

"I know," he said apologetically. "I just thought since he's only here two nights, it wouldn't be a big deal."

"It's a big deal." Jenna set the container down a little harder than necessary. "I have to record, and then I have to edit, and doing that with someone in the guest room makes me feel like I can't talk loud."

"You can still record," Liam said. He leaned against the counter, watching her. "He won't care."

"That's not the point," she said, shaking her head. "I wanted the house quiet. I have said that, like, three times this month."

"I just didn't want to tell him no," Liam said softly. "He's kind of scrambling right now."

"And I'm kind of scrambling," Jenna said, letting out a short breath. "I have a deadline on Monday, remember?"

Liam crossed the kitchen and opened the fridge to put away the milk even though it was already put away. "I can take him out Saturday," he said. "Get him out of your hair."

"That's . . . better," Jenna said slowly, "but I still have to plan around him."

"I said I'd handle it," Liam said, a little sharper now.

"I heard you," Jenna said defensively. "I'm telling you it still affects me" (generated by ChatGPT).

PAUSE HERE

Open your personalized workbook on your computer and review the practice exercise, asking

- What tags are unnecessary because the speaker is obvious?
- What adverbs are doing heavy lifting and should instead be shown through dialogue or action?
- What action beats unnecessarily state movement or comment on the dialogue rather than adding meaning?
- Are there too few or too many action beats?

After answering, revise the scene for better use of action beats and tags, then read my revision.

Problems with original:

This dialogue has too many tags and beats, given that it's clear who's speaking and that it's a high-tension scene. Several of the tags use adverbs, one action beat unnecessarily states movement, and the majority of tags and beats occur in the middle of the dialogue.

Revised:

"So . . . small thing," Liam said. "Evan's coming Friday."

Jenna looked up from the leftovers she was packing. "This Friday?"

"Yeah. He got the interview downtown and didn't want to pay for a hotel."

"Liam, I told you I wanted this weekend for the podcast stuff."

"I know. I just thought since he's only here two nights, it wouldn't be a big deal."

"It's a big deal." Jenna set the container down a little harder than necessary. "I have to record, and then I have to edit, and doing that with someone in the guest room makes me feel like I can't talk loud."

"You can still record. He won't care."

"That's not the point. I wanted the house quiet. I have said that, like, three times this month."

"I just didn't want to tell him no. He's kind of scrambling right now."

Jenna let out a short breath. "And I'm kind of scrambling. I have a deadline on Monday, remember?"

"I can take him out Saturday. Get him out of your hair," he said, putting the milk away.

"That's . . . better, but I still have to plan around him."

"I said I'd handle it."

"I heard you. I'm telling you it still affects me."

I got rid of unnecessary tags, varied the tag and beat placement, and removed the unnecessary movement: "crossed to the kitchen and opened the fridge."

EDITING STEPS

❑ Revise action beats and dialogue tags to ensure
- a good balance of beats and tags with a variety of placements
- minimal to no tagging when it's clear who's speaking
- limited to no adverbs
- action beats don't state unnecessary movement, unnecessary body parts, or what the dialogue or exposition already made clear
- variety of action beats rather than an overreliance on crutches

Words and Sentences

Strengthen Word Choice

You could improve the word choice of nearly every sentence in your manuscript, but doing that would be overwhelming. So focus on those quick wins—those easy fixes—that'll make your word choice much stronger.

Filter words

Filter words distance the reader from the character's lived experience, so you'll want to eliminate as many as you can. Since this topic also affects narrative distance, I addressed it in that topic as well. Go to page 143 to read the full explanation and examples.

Body parts

You can make two mistakes with body parts: making the body part do the action and unnecessarily naming the body part.

Making body part do the action:

Her hand reached for the keys in her pocket.

Really? Her hand had a mind of its own and did that? Nah. She did. This is an example of making the body part do the action.

As my copyediting fiction teacher, Jennifer Lawler, said, "By writing sentences that are ever-so-slightly inaccurate, you're ever-so-slightly distancing the reader from the moment."

Unnecessarily naming the body part:

> He took his sunglasses off his eyes.

> *You don't need to name the body part. We all know where sunglasses go.*

The most famous examples of unnecessarily naming a body part are "He shrugged his shoulders" and "she nodded her head." What else does one shrug or nod?

False simultaneity

Be careful of constructing sentences that sound like two things are happening at the same time when that couldn't actually be possible.

> Original: Opening the door, she rushed down the steps.

> Revised: After opening the door, she rushed down the steps.

She can't run down the stairs at the same time she's opening the door, but that's how the original sentence reads.

> Original: Watching intently for a mouse, the cat settled in to wait.

A cat can wait and watch at the same time, so this one is fine.

> Original: I strode out the door, hopping on my bicycle.

> Revised: I strode out the door, then hopped on my bicycle.

One can't walk out the door and get on their bike at the same time.

False simultaneity often occurs when you use an –ing word. So look at sentences that use an –ing verb, either at the start or at the end, and see if you created a false simultaneity.

You should also look for the words "as" and "while," which indicate something is happening at the same time.

Original:

- As she grabbed her backpack, she stuffed her notebook inside.
- She grabbed her backpack while she stuffed her notebook inside.

She can't grab her backpack and stuff her notebook inside at the same time.

Revised:

After grabbing her backpack, she stuffed her notebook inside.

Reduce wordiness

We all get wordy sometimes. I'm the wordiness queen—just ask my husband. Even though I struggle to stay concise, I can still edit out wordiness in others' writing. Before we start, let's clarify upfront: Reducing wordiness isn't just about shortening long sentences. Long sentences aren't automatically wordy; they can be powerful when used well. Wordiness often occurs when sentences rely on lots of little or unnecessary words, and this can also occur in short sentences.

So don't avoid long sentences—just make sure every word earns its place.

WORDS AND PHRASES TO CUT

Qualifiers: Words like "really," "quite," "often," etc. aren't always necessary.

Original sentence: She felt really afraid.
Revised options: She felt terrified. She felt afraid.

Prepositional phrases: Prepositions show location, time, and place: "of," "under," "from," "above," "at," etc. You can often replace prepositional phrases with one-word modifiers or reword them to avoid using them.

Original 16 words: The captain **of the starship** decided to launch an attack **on the enemy fleet at dawn.**

Revised 9 words: The starship captain attacked the enemy fleet at dawn.

Nominalizations (using verbs or adjectives as nouns): These words often end in "-ion," "-ment," "-ity/ty," or "-ness." To reduce wordiness, convert nominalizations into verbs.

Original 9 words: Marcus made the **decision** to confront the killer alone.

Revised 7 words: Marcus **decided** to confront the killer alone.

But remember, "decided to" is a filter word, so better to just say Marcus confronted the killer alone.

Original 13 words: It is my **recommendation** that Elena stay hidden until the guards pass by.

Revised 9 words: I **recommend** Elena stay hidden until the guards pass.

Adjectivizations (using verbs as adjectives): Convert them to verbs.

Original 12 words: The detective **was successful** in solving the case before the mayor's deadline.

Revised 11 words: The detective **succeeded** in solving the case before the mayor's deadline.

Expletive constructions: Expletives serve no grammatical function: there are, there is, it is, it was. Sometimes they're the best choice but not always.

Original 8 words: **There were** bloodstains splattered all over the walls.

Revised 4 words: Bloodstains splattered the walls.

Original 6 words: **It was** impossible to trust him.

Revised 4 words: Trusting him was impossible.

Which or that constructions: Omit "which" or "that" phrases when possible.

Original 12 words: The mansion, **which was old and crumbling**, held secrets from generations past.

Revised 9 words: The old, crumbling mansion held secrets from generations past.

Original 11 words: The sword **that was forged in dragon fire** glowed with power.

Revised 7 words: The dragon-forged sword glowed with power.

COMBINING SENTENCES TO REDUCE WORDINESS

You can combine sentences when using "this" to refer to the previous sentence.

Original 16 words: Sarah discovered the hidden passage. **This allowed** her to escape the castle before the guards arrived.

Revised 13 words: Sarah discovered the hidden passage**, allowing** her to escape before the guards arrived.

You can also combine sentences by using colons or –ing words or by omitting unnecessary parts.

Revised using colon:

Original 20 words: The wizard's spellbook contained seven forbidden incantations. **These spells were** Shadowbind, Soulfire, Eternal Night, Blood Mirror, Voidcall, Deathwhisper, and Mindshatter.

Revised 17 words: The wizard's spellbook contained seven forbidden incantations**:** Shadowbind, Soulfire, Eternal Night, Blood Mirror, Voidcall, Deathwhisper, and Mindshatter.

Revised using –ing word:

Original 13 words: The crowd scattered in different directions. **There were now** only two fighters remaining.

Revised 10 words: The crowd scattered in different directions, **leaving** only two fighters.

Revised through omission:

Original 29 words: Elena felt confused **about her feelings for James. Her confusion intensified** when she tried to understand his cryptic messages, decode his strange behavior, and figure out his true intentions.

Revised 16 words: Elena couldn't understand James's cryptic messages, decode his strange behavior, or figure out his true intentions.

Self-editing in practice

Original A:

> Evelyn realized the house was darker than she expected. She felt a chill creeping up her arms as she stepped inside. Her eyes darted around the foyer, searching for the source of the draft. Her hand fumbled with the light switch on the wall, but nothing happened. She knew the electricity must have been cut off.
>
> Opening the cellar door, she climbed down the narrow stairs. Listening for any further noises, she waited at the bottom of the steps. Her fingers tightened around the flashlight in her hand, and she lifted it in front of her face (generated by ChatGPT).

PAUSE HERE

Open your personalized workbook on your computer and review the practice exercise, asking

- If you deleted the filter word, what physical action or thought could replace it?
- Are any body parts doing the actions?
- Where are body parts named unnecessarily?
- Which sentences suggest two actions happening at the same time that couldn't be true?

After answering, revise the scene for word choice issues, then check my revision.

Problems with original A:

This passage contains all three word-choice issues. It uses filter words, names body parts unnecessarily, makes a body part do an action, and has some false simultaneity.

Revised A:

> The house was darker than she expected. When she stepped inside, a chill crept up her arms. Taking in the foyer, she searched for the source of the draft. She fumbled with the light switch on the wall, but nothing happened. The electricity must have been cut off.
>
> She opened the cellar door and climbed down the narrow stairs. Staying alert for any further noises, she waited at the bottom of the steps, gripped the flashlight, and lifted it in front of her.

My revision removed the filter words "realized," "felt," "knew," and "listening." I fixed the issue of her eyes and hand performing an action ("her eyes darted" and "her hand fumbled") and unnecessarily naming her hand as the body part holding the flashlight. Lastly, I fixed the one false simultaneity: opening a door and climbing down at the same time.

Original B:

> There was a darkness that seemed to really settle over the village at night, which was something that made the villagers significantly afraid to venture outside after sunset. It was a fact that they had developed an understanding that strange creatures were known to appear in the shadows. There were many different theories that existed about what these beings were, but it was not necessary to know the truth to feel the terror. A clear sense of caution in one's movements was something that could mean the difference between life and death.

> ## PAUSE HERE
>
> - What type of unnecessary words and phrases did you spot in the passage?
> - If you had to cut 25–30 percent of the words in this passage without losing meaning, what would you remove or condense?
>
> After answering, revise the passage to fix wordiness issues before reviewing mine.

Problems with original (word count 92) B:

The passage uses qualifiers, expletive constructions, nominalizations, prepositional phrases, and a "which" clause.

Revised B:

> Darkness settled over the village at night, making the villagers afraid to venture outside after sunset, as strange creatures appeared in the shadows. Many people theorized what those beings were, whispering their thoughts in the town. But the truth didn't matter. The fear did. Moving cautiously could mean the difference between life and death.

By eliminating qualifiers, expletive constructions, nominalizations, prepositional phrases, and "which" clauses, I decreased the word count to 54, a 41 percent reduction.

EDITING STEPS

❏ Use the Find feature in Word to search for common filter words and revise to eliminate them, unless their use is intentional to create a wider narrative distance.

❏ Stop when you encounter a body part and ask if you're unnecessarily naming it or if it's doing the action. If so, revise to fix that.

❏ Stop on sentences that use –ing verbs, "as," and "while" and make sure you haven't created any false simultaneity. Revise if so.

❏ Stop when a sentence (even short ones) feels like a mouthful and/or has several little words, and revise to avoid

- qualifiers
- prepositional phrases
- nominalizations
- adjectivizations
- expletive constructions
- unnecessary "which" or "that"

❏ Combine sentences that use "this" at the beginning of the second sentence.

❏ Check for sentence pairs you can combine using a colon and –ing word or by trimming portions.

Ensure Good Sentence Fluency

Remember the "dry eyes" guy? The "Bueller" guy? Same one. Look, his signature deadpan delivery may be funny, but it wouldn't work in writing. That lack of variety would decrease the narrative's fluidity if translated to text.

To increase your manuscript's fluidity, you need sentence variety—varying beginnings, length, and type. Such variety prevents monotony and repetitive rhythms.

Example:

> Darius opened the gate to the castle. Jessica followed close behind with her lantern. The guards stepped aside in silence. The courtyard stretched out before them. A black cat darted across their path. The bell in the tower tolled midnight.

> *Each sentence starts with the subject, follows a similar length, and relies on simple sentences.*

Monotony can still creep in when you vary some sentence elements but not others.

Vary sentence beginnings

Make sure your sentences start in different ways. Of course, don't start too many sentences in a row with the same word, but notice I said the same *way*, not the same *word*. In your manuscript, you likely will begin several sentences in a row the same way—it's a lengthy document, after all. But when a section doesn't flow well, reads flat, or has a repetitive rhythm, vary sentence beginnings to fix that.

SENTENCE PATTERN 1: BEGIN WITH THE SUBJECT

The most common sentence pattern starts with the subject (who or what the sentence is about).

> **My daughter** loves to spin in circles.

> **This story** is driving me up the wall.

SENTENCE PATTERN 2: BEGIN WITH A PREPOSITIONAL PHRASE

A preposition shows direction, location, or time.

> **Over on the other side of the bridge**, I saw a lone man walking toward me.

> **Along the way**, we learn many great life lessons.

SENTENCE PATTERN 3: BEGIN WITH A PARTICIPLE OR PARTICIPIAL PHRASE

A participle is a verb that ends in –ing or –ed.

Feeling a little tired, I had put my tablet aside and started to doze off when my cat jumped on me, jolting me awake.

Wracked with sorrow, I left without saying a word.

> **Problems to avoid**
>
> When you use sentence pattern 3, watch out for dangling modifiers: *Walking to work, a police car whizzed by.* This makes it sound like the police car was the one walking. After the participial phrase, the subject (the doer) should come first.
>
> You also need to watch out for creating false simultaneity: *Getting up out of the chair, he walked to the front door.* These actions can't both happen at the same time.

SENTENCE PATTERN 4: BEGIN WITH A DEPENDENT CLAUSE

A dependent clause starts with a subordinating conjunction, a connecting word that bridges the complete sentence to the partial sentence.

Because it rained, we had to cancel the party.

While I was taking the test, my pen ran out of ink.

SENTENCE PATTERN 5: BEGIN WITH AN APPOSITIVE

An appositive is a noun phrase that describes another noun.

A well-respected mayor, Bill knew he could run for president.

A struggling magician, Tom wandered from street to street.

SENTENCE PATTERN 6: BEGIN WITH AN INFINITIVE PHRASE

An infinitive is the word "to" plus a verb.

> **To be successful**, I had to start spending some money and investing in this.

> **To reduce my time on social media,** I blocked Facebook messages from appearing on my phone.

SENTENCE PATTERN 7: BEGIN WITH A SINGLE-WORD MODIFIER

A single-word modifier is one word that modifies the meaning of a word, clause, or phrase.

> **Happily**, she skipped to her room.

If you use the same sentence beginning pattern too many times in a row, it can make your narrative feel monotonous.

Original (from a manuscript I edited with names of characters changed):

> "Marcos again realized just how large of a man Stavier was. He must have been at least six feet tall and two hundred and fifty pounds. Stavier was wearing what Marcos remembered as a 'wife-beater' shirt—at least that's what the high school kids had called them. He thought those shirts looked just as trashy now as they did back then.

> "Stavier was completely bald with some black daggers tattooed on both sides of his head. His pants were skin-tight and clearly custom sewn.

"This guy has some massive thighs, and reminded Marcos of Zangief, from the old Street Fighter game.

"Stavier's rusty .45-caliber HK handgun was attached to his belt. It looked like a ten-round clip. Marcos fixed his gaze on Stavier's arms.

"Holy massive meat cleavers.

"Stavier's right arm had a tattoo. It was a number—'1985.' Marcos's eyes moved to Stavier's chest. *Someone has been juicing.* Stavier was an idiot, but not an idiot you would want to get in a fistfight with.

"Marcos suddenly felt embarrassed about eyeballing Stavier so thoroughly."

Original contains sixteen sentences in a row beginning with a subject. Even though the sentence lengths and types vary, the passage still feels a bit monotonous, choppy, and stilted.

Revised:

Man, Stavier was large. He must have been at least six feet tall and two hundred and fifty pounds. He was wearing what Marcos remembered as a "wifebeater" shirt—at least that's what the high school kids had called them. Those shirts looked just as trashy now as they did back then.

To complete his intimidating ensemble, Stavier was completely bald with three black daggers tattooed on both sides of his head. His pants were skin-tight and clearly custom sewn, with large leather stitches running up the sides. The guy had some massive thighs and reminded Marcos of Zangief, from the old Street Fighter game. Stavier's rusty .45-caliber HK handgun was attached to his belt. It looked like a ten-round clip. Marcos looked up, away from the gun. Staring at Stavier's arms, he gulped.

Holy massive meat cleavers.

His right arm had a tattoo, the number "1985." Marcos looked to Stavier's chest. Someone had been juicing. Yeah, Stavier was an idiot, but not an idiot you would want to get in a fistfight with.

Marcos let out a half-chuckle, half-grunt and turned away, stopping his intense observation of the man.

My revision now uses a single-word modifier, three sentences beginning with a subject, an infinitive phrase, five sentences starting with the subject, a participial phrase, three sentences beginning with a subject, a single-word modifier, and then a sentence starting with the subject.

Example:

"They (his gifts) certainly occupied us in the short term, but perhaps not as John intended. Ben appropriated the iPad, and I spent hours standing under the umbrella in the garden, shivering, shocked, while the new Cath Kidston Christmas slippers my sister had sent me got rain-soaked and muddy, and the puppy worked relentlessly to pull up a clematis when I should have been encouraging it to pee.

"Katrina lured John away from us just ten months before Ben disappeared. I thought of it as a master plan that she executed: The Seduction and Theft of My Husband. I didn't know the details of how they kindled their affair, but to me it felt like a plot from a bad medical drama. He had the real-life role of consultant pediatric surgeon; she was a newly qualified nutritionist.

"I imagined them meeting at a patient's bedside, eyes locking, hands grazing, a flirtation that turned into something more serious, until she offered herself to him unconditionally, the way you can before you have a child to consider" (From *What She Knew* by Gilly Macmillan).

Even though this contains several sentences in a row that start with the subject, the flow is fine, so I would leave it as is.

Sentence length and type

As I mentioned at the start of this topic, even if you vary your sentence beginnings, you might be using the same sentence type too often.

SIMPLE SENTENCE

A simple sentence is one complete thought.

The cat slept on the couch.

My brother and I went to the park and played soccer.

Sentences don't have to begin with the subject to be a simple sentence.

On the windowsill, the cat naps peacefully.

Every morning, birds chirp outside my window.

COMPOUND SENTENCE

A compound sentence has two or more complete thoughts (simple sentences) joined by a coordinating conjunction (FANBOYS: for, and, nor, but, or, yet, so) or a semicolon.

I wanted to go for a walk, but it started raining.

She likes tea; he prefers coffee.

Every morning birds chirp outside my window, and my dog barks at them.

COMPLEX SENTENCE

A complex sentence has one complete thought and at least one incomplete thought with a subordinating conjunction (because, although, since, if, when) or a relative pronoun (who, which) connecting them.

Because I was late (incomplete thought), I missed the meeting (complete thought).

I'll call you (complete thought) when I arrive (incomplete thought).

COMPOUND-COMPLEX SENTENCE

A compound-complex sentence has at least two complete thoughts and at least one incomplete thought. It combines features of compound and complex sentences.

Examples:

Although I was tired (incomplete thought), I finished my homework (complete thought), **and** I went to bed (complete thought).

She didn't come (complete thought) because she was sick (incomplete thought), **but** she sent a message (complete thought).

Let's look at how a passage can read when the sentence type isn't varied.

Original:

> The forest pressed close around her. Never before had Lila felt so small. Beneath the trees, shadows twisted and shifted. Suddenly, an owl screeched overhead. Most nights, the sound wouldn't have startled her. Tonight, it made her stumble. She tightened her grip on the lantern.
>
> Fortunately, the path was still visible. She could follow it until dawn. After that, the village would be safe again (generated by ChatGPT).

Seven sentences don't start with the subject, so you have sentence beginning variety here; however, they're all simple sentences, making the passage sound choppy.

Revised:

> The forest pressed close around her. Never before had Lila felt so small. Beneath the trees, shadows twisted and shifted while an owl screeched overhead (complex). Most nights, the sound wouldn't have startled her, but tonight, it made her stumble (compound). She tightened her grip on the lantern.
>
> Fortunately, the path was still visible. She could follow it until dawn, and after that, the village would be safe again (compound).

Still has the varied sentence beginnings, but now it also includes some compound and complex sentences.

Self-editing in practice

Original:

> Aria pushed the tavern door open and stepped into the smoky room. Patrons paused mid-drink to study her muddy cloak. She gulped. A fire popped in the hearth. The sparks went up the chimney. Barkeep Jonas raised an eyebrow but kept polishing a glass. A minstrel plucked a soft tune on his lute. Ale and sweat mingled in the air. A thief in the corner leaned forward with sudden interest (generated by ChatGPT).

PAUSE HERE

Open your personalized workbook on your computer and review the practice exercise, asking

- When you read this aloud, does it have a strong, varied rhythm, or does it feel a bit "samey"?

- Do several sentences start similarly or follow the same basic pattern?

- Are most of the sentences roughly the same length and type, or do you hear a mix of shorter/longer and different structures?

After answering, revise the passage for better sentence fluency before reading my revision.

Problems with original:

Every sentence is a simple sentence that starts with the subject, and nearly all are the same length.

Revised version:

> Aria pushed the tavern door open. When she stepped into the smoky room, patrons paused mid-drink to study her muddy cloak. She gulped just as a fire popped in the hearth, sending sparks up the chimney. Sneaking a glance at Jonas, she willed him to do something, but he kept polishing the glass. A minstrel plucked a soft tune on his lute, giving some life to the room full of ale and sweat. She took a hesitant step. A thief in the corner leaned forward with sudden interest.

Now two sentences no longer begin with the subject, and I used simple, compound, and complex sentences.

EDITING STEPS

❑ Pause when a section sounds flat, repetitive, or monotonous. (Don't just look at one paragraph. Read multiple paragraphs in the section to detect hidden rhythm issues.)

❑ Check your sentence beginnings: Do too many in a row follow the same beginning pattern even if the first word varies?

❑ Check the sentence lengths and types: Are most of the sentences the same length? Do they follow the same type?

❑ Revise with intentional variety if you answered yes to any of the above questions.

Eliminate Excess "Be" Verbs

William Zinsser said, "Use active verbs unless there's no comfortable way to get around using a passive verb."[7]

"Be" verbs aren't active verbs, and newer writers tend to overuse them. (Although let's clear up a common misconception: Using "be" verbs doesn't automatically mean you have passive voice.) "Be" verbs describe state of being:

- Is
- Am
- Are
- Was
- Were
- Be
- Being
- Been

These words aren't always bad, but they're weaker than active, powerful verbs. And beginning writers tend to overuse them. Also, be verbs cause sentences to be more wordy than needed.

Watch what happens when I rewrite the previous paragraph without "be" verbs: Despite sometimes needing "be" verbs, strong writers revise sentences to use more active, powerful verbs. This trims unnecessary words.

(Do you see what I did there? I eliminated the "be" verbs from the section explaining "be" verbs. I know . . . so clever.)

---

7   William Zinsser, *On Writing Well: The Classic Guide to Writing Nonfiction*, 30th anniversary ed. (New York: HarperCollins, 2006), 67.

You don't need to eliminate "be" verbs entirely. You just don't want to overuse them. Keep the "be" verb if revising around it would change the sentence's meaning, weaken the passage, or make the sentence clunky. Total elimination isn't the goal. Improving your writing is.

Methods to reduce "be" verbs

You can use these strategies to reduce "be" verbs when needed.

1. Change the main verb from an –ing to a regular verb. (But be careful: This does change the verb tense from past progressive to simple past, and sometimes you need the progressive tense for vibe, feeling, or accuracy.)

> Original: The moon was rising over the haunted castle.
>
> Revised: The moon rose over the haunted castle.

2. Change the "be" verb to a strong action verb.

> Original: Eliza is scared of the shadows in the attic.
>
> Revised: Eliza fears the shadows in the attic.

3. Write one or more showing sentence(s).

> Original: That alligator is aggressive.
>
> Revised: The alligator, angry at being disturbed, lurched forward and swallowed the boy's cat.

4. Rearrange the order of the sentence.

> Original: The monster was in the dark tunnel creeping.
>
> Revised: Down the dark tunnel crept the monster.

5. Combine sentences.

> Original: The knight was exhausted. He was lying on the battle-field, staring at the blood-red sky.

> Revised: The knight lay exhausted on the battlefield, staring at the blood-red sky.

6. Change another word to the verb.

> Original: Charles Schulz was the creator of the Peanuts cartoon strip.

> Revised: Charles Schulz created the Peanuts cartoon strip.

7. Get rid of unnecessary phrases.

> Original: She was trembling in the shadows because she was afraid of what might be waiting for her in the cellar.

> Revised: She trembled in the shadows, afraid of what waited in the cellar.

Examples

(These come from books I have edited.)

Original:

> "He **was** running through the forest, and his breath **was** coming in short, shallow gasps. His legs **were** burning from the climb, but he **was** afraid to slow down. Behind him, branches **were** snapping. He **was** certain the hunters **were** close enough to see him if he dared to look back."

Revised:

> As he ran through the forest, his breath came in short, shallow gasps. Even though his legs **were** burning from the climb, he had to keep going. He couldn't slow down. Not even for a second. Because then . . . well, he couldn't think about what would have happened then. With each snapping branch, he felt certain the hunters **were** close enough to see him if he dared to look back.

I changed the –ing verb (method 1), wrote one or more showing sentences (method 3), and combined sentences (method 5).

Original:

> "Maribel **was** the only one who **was** brave enough to step forward when the stranger appeared at the gate. The others **were** frozen in place, their eyes wide and their voices caught in their throats. Even the guards **were** standing back, as if the weight of the stranger's gaze **was** enough to keep them rooted where they **were**."

Revised:

> Maribel stepped forward when the stranger appeared at the gate. The others remained frozen in place, their eyes wide and their voices caught in their throats. Even the guards stood back, as if the weight of the stranger's gaze could keep them rooted in place.

I changed the verb to a stronger one—remained, could (method 2)—and got rid of unnecessary phrases—"was the only one who was brave enough to" and "where they were" (method 7).

Self-editing in practice

Original:

> The castle was sitting on the cliff, and mist was curling around its towers. Torches were flickering along the walls, but no guards were in sight. Inside, the great hall was filled with silence, as if the rooms were holding their breath (generated by ChatGPT).

> ## PAUSE HERE
>
> Open your personalized workbook on your computer and review the practice exercise, asking
>
> - How many "be" verbs (is, was, were, am, be, been, being) are in this passage?
> - Do any of those sentences feel vague, static, or wordy because of the "be" verb?
>
> After answering, rewrite to reduce the number of "be" verbs before reading my revision.

Problem with the original:

> The original has six "be" verbs, weakening the passage.

Revised:

> The castle perched on the cliff, mist curling around its towers. Torches flickered along the walls, but no guards appeared. Inside, silence filled the great hall, as if the rooms were holding their breath.

> *I changed the –ing verb (method 1), used stronger verbs (method 2), and rearranged the order of a sentence (method 4).*

EDITING STEPS

❑ Stop when a passage feels wordy, flat, or overly dependent on "be" verbs.

❑ Scan the section for an overuse of "be" verbs.

❑ Revise by reducing "be" verbs using any of the six strategies:
- Swap for a stronger verb
- Cut "be" verb and change –ing form of verb
- Show instead of tell
- Make another word in the sentence the verb
- Combine sentences
- Rearrange sentence order
- Get rid of unnecessary phrases

STOP: DON'T READ AHEAD YET

Apply the two or three topics you chose for this pass to your manuscript before moving on.

This book is a toolbox, not a linear book. You'll get the most value from doing the work *as you go*.

If you haven't done so yet, scan the QR code or visit: https://beaconpointservices.org/generate-fiction-personalized-workbook.

For best results, open on a computer or tablet to download and edit the Word document.

When you're ready, come back and begin the next pass.

You've got this.

TECHNICAL PASS

Grammar, spelling, and punctuation . . . I know, I know. This isn't the exciting part of writing. I'll try not to drag you back into a stuffy English class, but if you're going to be a writer, you need to know the basics.

If you were in my actual class, we would have so much fun with this: jokes galore, maybe some rapping or tap dancing, or even an interpretive dance about commas. But you're not in my actual classroom. You're reading a book. So I'll spare you the tap shoes and focus on what matters most: the minor tweaks that'll make the most significant difference.

During this pass, focus on fixing actual errors: grammar, spelling, capitalization, and punctuation mistakes that distract readers. Since comprehensive coverage of all the rules of grammar would make this guide overwhelming, I have focused on the most common errors I see in each category (spelling, punctuation, and grammar).

Start by doing the general find-and-replace tasks (they're quick wins). Then pick just two to three topics to read and apply in this pass, focusing on the ones your story needs most. Of course, you'll want to fix any errors you catch, but to start, just focus on the topics you chose.

Remember, I'm also developing a manuscript diagnostic tool designed to help authors pinpoint their highest-priority editing topics more quickly and accurately, using an editorial eye rather than an author's eye. In the meantime, I offer Manuscript Checkup services that provide personalized guidance to help you decide what to self-edit for. See appendix A to learn about both options.

Make sure to do the find-and-replace tasks (starts on page 250), then pick two or three topics from these options:

- Correct easily confused words (page 256)
- Ensure correct use of periods and commas with dialogue (page 267)
- Ensure correct use of ellipses and em dashes in dialogue (page 272)
- Fix common comma errors (page 279)
- Fix dangling modifiers (page 287)

Personalized workbook: To generate your customizable technical pass workbook, scan the QR code or visit https://beaconpointservices.org/generate-fiction-personalized-workbook.

For best results, open on a computer or tablet to download and edit the Word document.

Take Care of General Find-and-Replace Tasks

The easiest fixes take five minutes and a few clicks—if you know what to look for. They're just simple find-and-replace tasks. An editor can easily fix them too, but why leave it to them when you can easily just do the thing yourself?

The next few steps are quick Word tricks (I promise), and once you know them, you'll fly through cleanup. This topic differs from the rest because it doesn't include an editing practice or editing steps. The editing steps are simply to perform the find-and-replace tasks outlined below.

> **Software**
>
> While the screenshots and examples in this topic come from Word on a PC, all major word-processing programs have a find-and-replace feature.

To use find and replace, go to Find on the Word ribbon and select "Advanced Find."

This brings up a box with "Find what" and "Replace with." In the instructions below, anything in parentheses represents a button you press, not something to actually type in. So (space) would indicate you press the space bar, not type in "space."

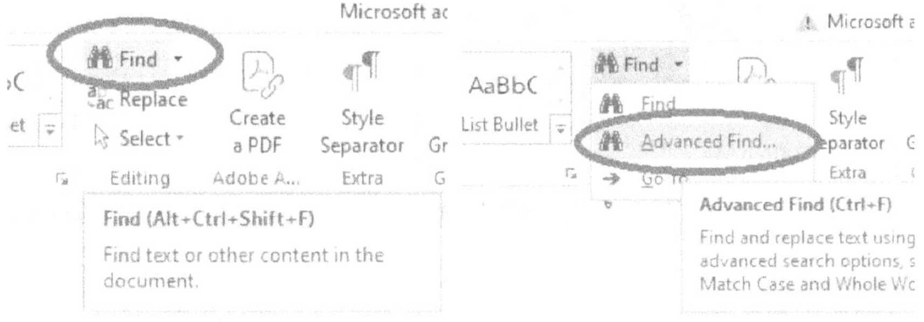

Eliminate double spaces after periods

Find what: (space)(space)

Replace with: (space)

You might have been taught to insert two spaces after a period. I was taught this way too, and I did struggle to break the habit at first. Back when typewriters were a thing, double spaces were necessary. Now, they aren't. So eliminating them is an easy win.

Tabbed indents

Find what: ^t

Replace with: [leave this blank]

Paragraphs shouldn't be indented by pressing "tab." When your book gets to the design stage, these indents won't transfer. Editors use Word Styles to get your paragraphs to indent automatically. Don't need to worry about Word Styles right now, but do get rid of any tabbed indents. If you want to include indents in your document without using Word Styles (your editor will apply those), then do the following:

Highlight your entire document by hitting Ctrl+A. Then, in the Paragraph section of the toolbar, click on the arrow in the right-hand corner. Or right-click (PC) or triple-click (Mac) to open the paragraph pop-up window.

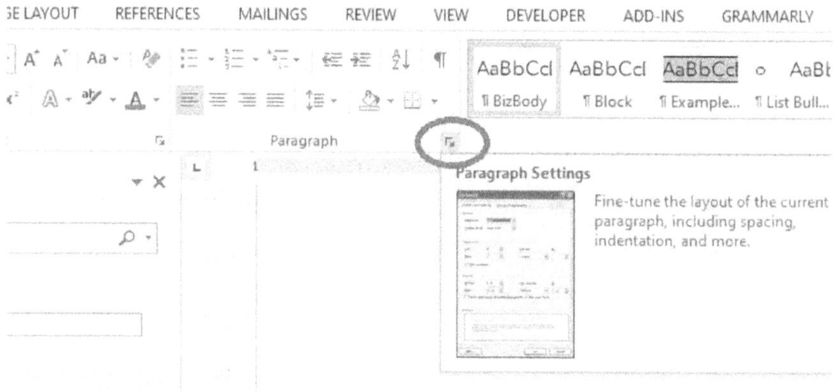

A dialogue box will pop up. Under "Special," select "First line." Under "By," select "0.5" (or whatever you want the indent to be, but this is the standard). Then click OK.

Straight quotes

First, make sure your document is set up to autocorrect straight quotes to smart quotes. This is the default setting, so it's most likely already the case. But just in case, go to File → Options → Proofing. Then click on the "Autocorrect Options" button. From there, select "Autoformat" and make sure "Change straight quotes to smart quotes" is selected.

Then, in the find-and-replace box, enter straight, not curly, quote marks.

For single quotes:

Find: '

Replace: '

For double quotes:

Find: "

Replace: "

Yes, you're typing the exact same thing in the find-and-replace box, but since it's set to autocorrect to curly (smart) quotes, it'll put in the correct ones.

Eliminate soft returns

Unless you intentionally put in a soft return (a manual line break), remove all soft returns. If you don't know what a soft return is, you most likely didn't use them on purpose.

Find what: ^l [that's a lowercase L]

Replace with: ^p [that's a paragraph break]

Change double returns to single

This will remove unnecessary spaces between paragraphs. You never want double returns in your document.

Find what: ^p^p

Replace with: ^p

Em and en dashes

If you're following the Chicago Manual of Style (CMoS), use em dashes, not en dashes, to surround parenthetical elements. If you're following

British style, use en dashes. CMoS recommends unspaced em dashes, but if you prefer to space them out, that's fine. Just let your editor know.

Example	How to change to this from unspaced hyphens	How to change to this from spaced hyphens	How to change to this from spaced en dash
Unspaced em dash My son—the cutest kid ever—has learned how to army crawl.	Find: - Replace: ^+	Find: (space)-(space) Replace: ^+	Find: (space)^=(space) Replace: ^+
Spaced em dash My son — the cutest kid ever — has learned to army crawl.	Find: - Replace: (space)^+(space)	Find: (space)-(space) Replace: (space)^+(space)	Find: (space)^=(space) Replace: (space) ^+(space)
Spaced en dash My son – the cutest kid ever – has learned to army crawl.	Find: - Replace: (space)^=(space)	Find: (space)-(space) Replace: (space)^=(space)	

Change hyphen between number to an en dash

With a range of numbers, use an en dash rather than a hyphen. So it should be 3–20, not 3-20.

Make sure you check the "Use wildcards" box, or this find and replace won't work. To enable wildcards, click on "More" and select "Use wildcards."

Find: ([0-9])-([0-9])

Replace: \1^=\2

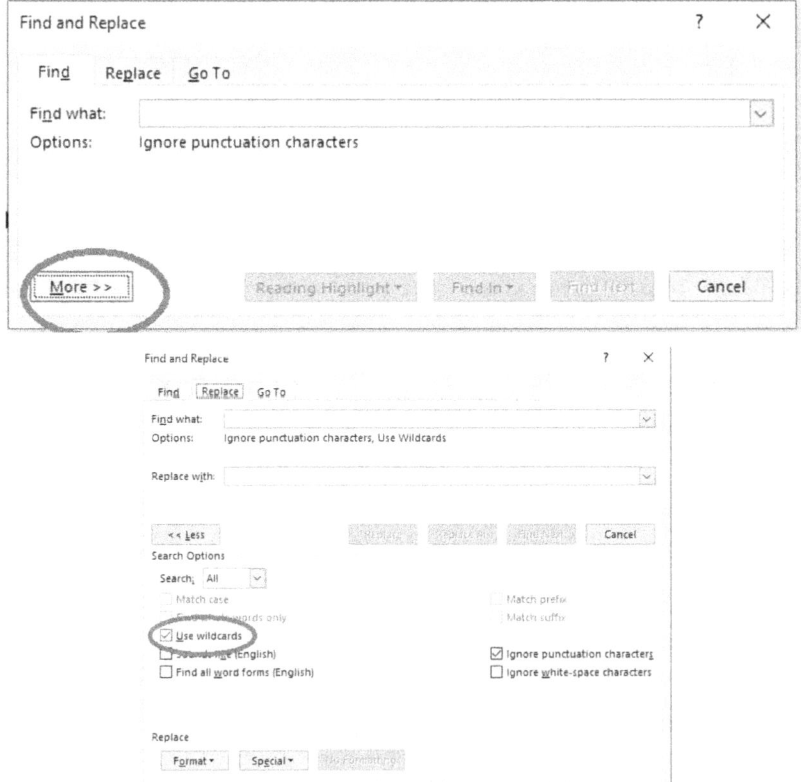

Once you run these quick fixes, your manuscript will be cleaner. Yay for easy wins!

Correct Easily Confused Words (Spelling)

I have a mortifying confession: I'm a professional editor, and I still mix up "lose" and "loose." I know the difference. I even *teach* the difference. But my fingers don't always cooperate with my brain.

Do you know your troublesome words too (to)? It's easier than (then?) you think to find and fix them. You're (your?) going to just use a few research skills and the Find feature in Word.

These little errors don't make you a bad writer. They just make your writing look less polished, and readers tend to assign credibility based on technical accuracy.

So let's walk through the most common offenders.

Please note, this isn't an all-inclusive list. I recommend Debbie Emmitt's *Tricky Quickies* series to learn more (see appendix B for the link to this and other resources).

Your/You're

Your = possessive → something belongs to you
You're = you are

Examples:

> Your example was excellent.

> You're doing a great job self-editing.

Quick tip: If you can replace the word with "you are," use "you're."

Their/There/They're

Their = possessive

There = location or a dummy subject ("There's . . .")

They're = they are

Examples:

> The team shared their results.

> Put the report over there.

> They're presenting tomorrow.

Quick tip: "They're" must always expand to "they are."

It's/Its

It's = it is

Its = possessive (yes, English likes chaos)

Examples:

> It's a great idea.

> The system updated its settings.

Quick tip: If you can't expand to "it is," you need "its."

Accept/Except

Accept = to receive or agree to

Except = excluding

Examples:

> I cannot accept that edit.

> Everyone attended except Jonathan.

Quick tip: If you can replace it with "receive," it's "accept."

Good/Well

Good = adjective → describes nouns
Well = adverb → describes actions

Examples:

> She wrote a good proposal.

> She writes well.

Quick tip: If it describes *how* someone does something → "well."

Into/In to

Into = movement/transformation
In to = the word in followed by to

Examples:

> She walked into the room.

> I logged in to update the file.

Quick tip: If you can swap the word with "inside," use "into."

Chose/Choose

Chose = past tense

Choose = present/future

Examples:

> Yesterday, I chose a topic.

> Today, I'll choose headings.

Lose/Loose

Lose = to misplace or be deprived of

Loose = not tight

Examples:

> I don't want to lose momentum.

> These pants are too loose.

Quick tip: Double O in "loose" → extra space → not tight.

Affect/Effect

Affect = verb, to influence

Effect = noun, a result

Examples:

> That comment didn't affect my edits.

> The effect was improved clarity.

Quick tip: "Affect" = action (both start with A). "Effect" = end result (both start with E).

Sell/Sale

Sell = verb
Sale = noun

Examples:

> I sell editing services.
>
> The book is on sale.

Quick tip: If you can put "a" or "the" before it, use "sale."

Principal/Principle

Principal = noun, main person in charge of a school; adjective, most important
Principle = rule, value, or concept

Examples:

> Our principal concern is clarity.
>
> It's a matter of principle.

Quick tip: Principal = PAL (your principal is your pal).

Advice/Advise

Advice = noun
Advise = verb

Examples:

> Thank you for the advice.
>
> I advise running a read-aloud pass.

Illicit/Elicit

Illicit = illegal

Elicit = to draw out

Examples:

That was an illicit document leak.

The story will elicit emotion.

Further/Farther

Further = metaphorical distance

Farther = physical distance

Examples:

Let's take this idea further.

She walked three miles farther.

Lay/Lie/Laid

Lay = present tense of "to lay" (requires an object)

Lay = past tense of "to lie" (no object)

Lie = to recline

Laid = past tense of lay

Examples:

I lay the book down.

I want to lie down.

I laid my keys by the door so I wouldn't forget them.

Yesterday I lay on the couch for an hour.

(This one consistently hurts people's souls. It's okay.)

Then/Than

Then = time
Than = comparison

Examples:

First we draft, then we revise.

Editing takes longer than most people expect.

Whether/Weather

Whether = choice
Weather = rain/sun/snow

Examples:

I'm deciding whether this chapter needs another example.

I love living in Utah but hate the weather.

Fewer/Less

Fewer = countable items
Less = mass quantity or uncountable concepts

Examples:

> This chapter has fewer examples than the last one.

> The new outline requires less work overall.

Complement/Compliment

Complement = completes
Compliment = praise

Examples:

> Your introduction complements the chapter beautifully.

> He complimented me on the structure of the final draft.

Self-editing in practice

Original A:

> I tried to accept the apology gracefully, except I couldn't stop thinking about the insult hidden in his words. I wasn't sure how much it would effect my trust in him, but I feared it might affect our friendship forever.

> Yesterday, I lay the blanket on the grass and asked Thomas to lay beside me while I went to lay down in the shade. Instead, he just lay in the dirt fiddling with sticks until supper.

> Your welcome to stay if you're not afraid of ghosts. Their probably not real, but the villagers swear there are already restless spirits in the manor.

The principle reason we choose this path was the promise of treasure, but now I wish we had chose differently. It's a matter of principal now, not just greed (generated by ChatGPT).

PAUSE HERE

Open your personalized workbook on your computer and correct the misspelled words, then check my revision for the answers.

Revised A:

I tried to accept the apology gracefully, except I couldn't stop thinking about the insult hidden in his words. I wasn't sure how much it would **affect** my trust in him, but I feared it might affect our friendship forever.

Yesterday, I **laid** the blanket on the grass and asked Thomas to **lie** beside me while I went to **lie** down in the shade. Instead, he just lay in the dirt fiddling with sticks until supper.

You're welcome to stay if you're not afraid of ghosts. **They're** probably not real, but the villagers swear there are already restless spirits in the manor.

The **principal** reason we **chose** this path was the promise of treasure, but now I wish we had **chosen** differently. It's a matter of **principle** now, not just greed.

Original B:

> She wanted to advise the knight on which road was safer, but he refused to take her advise. He worried more about the affect the delay would have on his honor rather than the effect it might have on his men's safety.
>
> He studied the notice board and said, "Wow, that's a great sale on swords." But I had to explain that the sign meant they wouldn't be for sell until market day. So I couldn't sale him one at that price today. He told me he wouldn't except that and stormed off.
>
> He marched further into the forest than any of the others, determined to further prove his bravery. He had less experience with monsters than his companions, but he had plenty of courage. He just wished less people were whispering behind him, especially his brother (generated by ChatGPT).

PAUSE HERE

Correct the misspelled words, then check my revision for the answers.

Revised B:

> She wanted to advise the knight on which road was safer, but he refused to take her **advice.** He worried more about the **effect** the delay would have on his honor rather than the effect it might have on his men's safety.
>
> He studied the notice board and said, "Wow, that's a great sale on swords." But I had to explain that the sign meant they wouldn't be

for **sale** until market day. So I couldn't **sell** him one at that price today. He told me he wouldn't **accept** that and stormed off.

He marched **farther** into the forest than any of the others, determined to further prove his bravery. He had less experience with monsters than his companions, but he had plenty of courage. He just wished **fewer** people were whispering behind him, especially his brother.

EDITING STEPS

- ❏ Use Word's Find feature to search for the first word in a pair you tend to confuse.
- ❏ For each result, check whether the word is used correctly in context.
- ❏ Search for the second word in the pair and review its usage.
- ❏ Repeat with each word pair you struggle with.

Ensure Correct Use of Periods and Commas with Dialogue (Punctuation)

When you have an actual dialogue tag—which must contain a verb of utterance—then you need to separate the dialogue from the tag with a comma.

- "Seriously, this restaurant has the best free chips and salsa," he said. (comma inside closing quotation mark before tag)
- He said, "Seriously, this restaurant has the best free chips and salsa." (comma after tag and before quotation mark)
- "Seriously," he said, "this restaurant has the best free chips and salsa." (comma on both sides of tag with first one inside closing quotation mark)

Another common issue is punctuating action beats as dialogue tags. An action beat is separated by a period, not a comma. If the action beat comes in the middle of the dialogue, it can be separated by a pair of em dashes or with periods.

- "Seriously, this restaurant has the best free chips and salsa." He rubbed his belly. (period inside closing quotation mark before action beat)
- He rubbed his belly. "Seriously, this restaurant has the best free chips and salsa." (period after action beat and before quotation mark)

- "Seriously"—he rubbed his belly—"this restaurant has the best free chips and salsa." (em dashes outside of quotation marks before and after the beat, showing he did the action while talking)
- "Seriously." He rubbed his belly. "This restaurant has the best free chips and salsa." (period inside quotation mark for the first half, then period after the action beat to show he did the action in between speaking)

Sometimes shorter action beats—those that only include the name or pronoun of the speaker and a single action—get mistaken for dialogue tags, which include just the name or pronoun of the speaker and the verb of utterance. But if you don't have a verb of utterance, you don't have a dialogue tag.

These words *aren't* verbs of utterance:

- Smiled
- Laughed
- Grinned
- Frowned
- Sighed
- Nodded
- Snickered
- Chuckled
- Groaned

So when you use these words, you need to have a period, not a comma.

"I didn't mean it," he groaned. = incorrect

"I didn't mean it." He groaned.

She laughed, "Sure, you didn't." = incorrect.

She laughed. "Sure, you didn't."

Some editors will say you can laugh or sigh a short line of dialogue. After all, we *do* laugh while talking. But really, you're not laughing the words; you're just doing two actions at the same time: laughing and talking.

I'm in the camp of never using these words as dialogue tags. You risk taking the reader out of the moment if they think, "How does one laugh words?" So I'm the editor who'll always punctuate these as action beats. Of course, my clients have complete control and can reject the change and decide they're in the camp of "one can laugh a few words." (For more on this, see a collaborative webinar I did with another editor, Dialogue Punctuation Rules: Everything You've Ever Wanted to Know on my website courses page.)

Self-editing in practice

Original:

"Are you really going to wear that?" Jenna asked, raising an eyebrow.

"I . . . I think so." Mark said.

"It's green. And you hate green."

"I know. But it was the only clean one," he grimaced.

"Clean doesn't mean it looks good." She laughed.

Mark ran a hand through his hair, scratching the back of his neck, "You're overreacting, as usual."

"You call this" she leaned closer, "overreacting?"

"I—well—I mean . . ."

Jenna rolled her eyes, "It's hideous."

"Stop staring at me like that."

She smirked, "Like what?"

Mark exhaled, shoulders sagging. "Like you're plotting something."

"Maybe I am" (generated by ChatGPT).

PAUSE HERE

Open your personalized workbook on your computer and review the practice exercise, asking

- Are any commas incorrectly connecting a line of dialogue to an action beat?

- Are there periods following a dialogue tag?

- Are there action beats inside a line of dialogue where a pair of em dashes would create a cleaner structure?

- For any verb used in a dialogue tag, ask, Can you literally speak while doing that verb?

After answering the questions, revise for correct punctuation, then read my revision.

Revised:

"Are you really going to wear that?" Jenna asked, raising an eyebrow.

"I . . . I think so," Mark said.

"It's green. And you hate green."

"I know. But it was the only clean one." He grimaced.

"Clean doesn't mean it looks good." She laughed.

Mark ran a hand through his hair, scratching the back of his neck. "You're overreacting, as usual."

"You call this"—she leaned closer—"overreacting?"

"I—well—I mean . . ."

Jenna rolled her eyes. "It's hideous."

"Stop staring at me like that."

She smirked. "Like what?"

Mark exhaled, shoulders sagging. "Like you're plotting something."

"Maybe I am."

EDITING STEPS

- ❏ Zoom in so you can easily see the punctuation.
- ❏ Change periods to commas when a dialogue tag appears before or after a line of dialogue.
- ❏ Change commas to periods if you have an action beat before or after a line of dialogue.
- ❏ Change any commas to em dashes or periods if you have an action beat in the middle of a line of dialogue.

Ensure Correct Use of Ellipses and Em Dashes in Dialogue (Punctuation)

Ellipses and em dashes are used in dialogue in specific ways, and authors commonly use the wrong one in a given situation.

Using ellipses

Use an ellipsis (…) when a speaker trails off or has an unintentional pause.

Whether you write the ellipsis closed up or with spaces (… versus . . .) is a matter of style. I like the second one, which follows the Chicago Manual of Style guidelines; some prefer the first. And some authors don't like to include a space before the first dot (like this…). No matter how you render your ellipses, make sure you're consistent.

Examples:

> "I don't . . . Listen, I really don't know."

Here, the speaker paused after "I don't." But it wasn't a pause that would naturally occur as we speak. It was an unintentional pause, a pause where they were gathering themselves together.

> "Do you think you could . . . ?"

Here, the speaker trails off and doesn't finish their thought.

If the punctuation already shows the pause or cutoff, you don't need to explain it in the action beat.

> "I don't"—he paused—"Listen, I really don't know."

> "Do you think you could . . . ?" He trailed off.

In both instances, the action beat should be deleted.

Using em dashes

Use an em dash (—) when a speaker is cut off either by themselves or by another speaker.

The em dash is longer than either a hyphen or an en dash. You create it by typing two hyphens with no spaces around them or by pressing Alt+0151 (use the numeric pad). If you don't have a numerical pad, use Ctrl + Alt + - (PC) or Option + Shift + - (Mac).

Examples:

> "I don't get—"

> "And you never will."

Here, the speaker was cut off by another speaker.

> "I don't get—Hey, wait, you were there?"

> "I don't get—" He stared at me, deep into my soul. "Wait, you were there?"

In both of these examples, the speaker cut themselves off.

Since the em dash shows a speaker has been cut off, you don't need to also state they were interrupted.

"I don't get—"

Lilly interrupted him. "And you never will."

Get rid of "Lilly interrupted him" and use the dash to show it.

If the action beat is the interruption, then, yes, you will state that.

"I don't get—"

Lilly slammed down the pot lid. "And you never will."

If you have an action beat with the speaker being interrupted, make sure it comes before the interrupted line of dialogue; otherwise, it disrupts the pulse of the dialogue.

"I don't get—" He sighed.

"And you never will."

This ruins the dialogue's pulse. Instead, change it to:

He sighed. "I don't get—"

"And you never will."

Self-editing in practice

Original:

"Are you sure about this plan?" Tahani asked, tapping her fingers on the table.

"Well, I think we should . . . I mean, what other choice do we have?"

"Wait, did you hear that—"

"Hear what? I don't hear anything unusual."

"Maybe we shouldn't go through with this." Tahani ran her hand through her hair nervously.

"Listen, I know what you're thinking, but . . ." Tom was interrupted by a loud crash from upstairs.

"Oh, great. Now what?"

"I was trying to tell you that I saw someone watching the house earlier."

"You saw someone—Why didn't you mention this before?"

"I thought. I thought maybe I was just being paranoid."

"Being paranoid is better than being dead, Tom."

"Look, we can either stay here and wait, or—" He stopped mid-sentence, staring at the window.

"Or what? Tom, you're scaring me . . ."

"The lights just went out across the street."

"This could mean—"(generated by ChatGPT).

PAUSE HERE

Open your personalized workbook on your computer and review the practice exercise, asking

- Is the speaker trailing off or hesitating? (If yes, you should use an ellipsis.)

- Is the speaker being cut off by themselves or someone else? (If yes, you should use an em dash.)

- Does any action beat repeat what the punctuation already shows? (If yes, delete or move it.)

After making the needed changes, read my revision.

Revised:

"Are you sure about this plan?" Tahani asked, tapping her fingers on the table.

"Well, I think we should—I mean, what other choice do we have?"

"Wait, did you hear that—"

"Hear what? I don't hear anything unusual."

"Maybe we shouldn't go through with this." Tahani ran her hand through her hair nervously.

"Listen, I know what you're thinking, but—"

A loud crash came from upstairs.

I changed ellipses to an em dash and removed "Tom was interrupted" since the em dash shows that.

"Oh, great. Now what?"

"I was trying to tell you that I saw someone watching the house earlier."

"You saw someone? Why didn't you mention this before?"

No cutting off is happening here, so I removed the em dash.

"I thought . . . I thought maybe I was just being paranoid."

Since this is an unintentional pause while the character gathers their thoughts, I put in an ellipsis.

"Being paranoid is better than being dead, Tom."

He stared at the window. "Look, we can either stay here and wait, or—"

"Or what? Tom, you're scaring me."

Moved the action beat so it didn't interrupt the interruption and deleted the ellipsis since it's not a trailed-off thought.

"The lights just went out across the street."

"This could mean . . ."

Changed to an ellipsis since it's an incomplete thought, but the character is not being interrupted.

EDITING STEPS

- ❑ Find dialogue where you intended to show trailing off or an unintentional pause, and ensure you use ellipses.
- ❑ Find dialogue where you intended to show a speaker was interrupted either by another speaker or themselves, and ensure you use the em dash.
- ❑ Get rid of action beats that state the speaker trailed off or was interrupted, since the punctuation already shows that.
- ❑ Ensure any necessary action beat comes before, not after, the interrupted line of dialogue.

Fix Common Comma Errors (Punctuation)

Commas are a pain, and I say that as an editor. We editors constantly ask each other comma questions, and we debate what's correct more than you'd think. So if even professional editors can't always agree on commas, you shouldn't feel discouraged when you struggle with them!

But here's the good news: Despite dozens of comma rules, most manuscripts see the same four errors over and over: comma splice, run-on, introductory error, and fused sentence. Master these four, and you'll catch the majority of your comma problems.

Commas with coordinating conjunctions (comma splices and run-ons)

Let's call these conjunctions FANBOYS: for, and, nor, but, or, yet, so. These words join parts of sentences and have clear rules for when you need a comma.

Rule 1. When a FANBOYS word joins phrases, skip the comma—though you may choose to add one for stylistic reasons.

Rule 2. When a FANBOYS word joins independent clauses, include the comma. You can't have just a comma between two sentences, nor can you rely on just the FANBOYS. You need both.

Clause example:

> Kai lifted his sword, but his hands still trembled.

Both clauses could be sentences by themselves. Kai lifted his sword. His hands still trembled. So, since a FANBOYS is joining them, you need that comma before "but."

Phrase example:

> Kai lifted his sword but didn't strike.

"Didn't strike" is a phrase since it doesn't contain a subject, so no comma is required before the "but."

Error 1. Comma splice (comma but no FANBOYS):

> Lila hated the dark, it always made her heart race.

Fix options:

> Lila hated the dark. It always made her heart race.

> Lila hated the dark, **for** it always made her heart race.

Error 2. Run-on (FANBOYS but no comma):

> The villagers tried to sleep but the howling kept them awake

Fix:

> The villagers tried to sleep, but the howling kept them awake.

Fused sentences

You have three ways to join two or more independent clauses. Of course, you can just use a period and create separate sentences. But if you opt to join the clauses, use one of these three methods: Both a comma and a FANBOYS, a semicolon, or, in certain situations, a colon. But with no punctuation between two independent clauses, you have a fused sentence.

> Fused sentence: The wind rattled the shutters it made the cabin feel more alive.

> Correct: The wind rattled the shutters, **and** it made the cabin feel more alive.

> Correct: The wind rattled the shutters; it made the cabin feel more alive.

Commas with introductions

A comma usually goes after sentence introductions (a word, clause, or phrase that comes before the independent clause).

SINGLE-WORD

One word that modifies the meaning of an entire clause.

> Surprisingly, the roof was still intact.

You need a comma after your one word sentence introduction.

The exception to this is when the one-word sentence introduction indicates when something happened.

> Often I snack in the afternoon.

No comma needed after "often."

SUBORDINATING CLAUSE

Subordinating clauses begin with a subordinating conjunction (after, although, as, when, while, until, unless, before, because, if, since) and don't express a complete thought.

Although the storm raged outside, Mara kept writing by candlelight.

"Although the storm raged outside" contains a subject (storm) and verb (raged), but it doesn't express a complete thought. It begins with a subordinating conjunction (although). Comma goes at the end of the dependent clause and before the main clause: Mara kept writing by candlelight.

INFINITIVE PHRASE

An infinitive phrase begins with the infinitive form of the verb (to + base form).

To win the duel, Aaron had to steady his breathing.

Begins with to + verb (win) and doesn't contain a subject. Comma goes at the end of the entire infinitive phrase and before the main clause: Aaron had to steady his breathing.

> **Tip**
>
> Watch out for sentences where the infinitive phrase functions as the subject of the sentence: To start a new business without doing market research and long-term planning in advance would be foolish. (No comma between "advance" and "would" because it doesn't function as an introductory phrase—it acts as the subject of the sentence.)

PARTICIPIAL PHRASE

A participial phrase begins with a past or present participle (–ed or –ing form of a verb that functions as an adjective).

Shaking with fury, the knight lowered his visor.

Begins with a present participle (shaking). Comma goes at the end of the entire participial phrase and before the main clause: the knight lowered his visor.

> **Tip**
>
> Don't confuse a participle with a gerund (an –ing verb functioning as a noun): Singing and dancing at the same time is hard to do. (No comma here because *singing* and *dancing* function as nouns, not adjectives, and serve as the sentence's subject.)

PREPOSITIONAL PHRASE

A prepositional phrase begins with a preposition, a word that indicates position (about, above, across, after, over, under, near, etc.).

Under the pale moonlight, the forest seemed endless.

Begins with a preposition (under). Comma goes at the end of the prepositional phrase and before the main clause: the forest seemed endless.

No comma needed after a short prepositional phrase (two to three words), though you can add one for stylistic purposes.

ABSOLUTE PHRASE

An absolute phrase has a noun and modifiers and often includes a participle, but not always.

His courage restored, Jalen marched into the throne room.

His courage (noun) restored (participle). Comma goes at the end of the entire absolute phrase and before the main clause: Jalen marched into the throne room.

Self-editing in practice

Original:

Rain streaked the windowpanes, painting the world in blurred lines.

Lila hated the dark, it always made her chest tighten. She sat on the floor with her back against the cold wall, holding the lantern so its light pooled at her knees. Footprints led through the muddy yard someone had climbed over the low hedge recently.

She relit the lantern but the flame guttered and died. She cursed under her breath and knelt to cup a new match between careful fingers. Just then a scream pierced the air.

After the scream passed she steadied herself and tried to listen for any sign that someone remained outside. For a long moment only the rain answered.

Then, very slowly, the latch on the back door clicked. The dog, who had been sleeping, bolted upright and barked once.

Lila swallowed hard and forced a laugh even though her voice shook (generated by ChatGPT).

> **PAUSE HERE**
>
> Open your personalized workbook on your computer and correct the common comma errors, then read my revision.

Revised:

(Note that many comma errors can be fixed in multiple ways. So your fix may be different than mine.)

Rain streaked the windowpanes, painting the world in blurred lines.

Lila hated the dark. It always made her chest tighten. She sat on the floor with her back against the cold wall and held the lantern so its light pooled at her knees. Footprints led through the muddy yard, and someone had climbed over the low hedge recently.

She relit the lantern, but the flame guttered and died. She cursed under her breath and knelt to cup a new match between careful fingers. Just then a scream pierced the air.

After the scream passed, she steadied herself and tried to listen for any sign that someone remained outside. For a long moment only the rain answered.

Then, very slowly, the latch on the back door clicked. The dog, who had been sleeping, bolted upright and barked once.

Lila swallowed hard and forced a laugh even though her voice shook.

EDITING STEPS

❑ Watch out for run-ons. Check all coordinating conjunctions (FANBOYS) between two clauses. If each side could stand alone as its own sentence, insert a comma before the FANBOYS. If one side is a phrase (not a complete sentence), a comma usually isn't needed, though you can stylistically choose to have one.

❑ Watch out for comma splices. If two sentences are joined with just a comma, fix it by adding the missing FANBOYS or make it a period.

❑ Watch out for fused sentences. If two sentences aren't joined by anything, fix it by using one of the correct methods (comma and FANBOYS, semicolon, colon) or split it into two sentences with a period.

❑ Look at sentences with introductory words, clauses, or phrases. If a sentence starts with something before the main subject-verb clause, check if it needs a comma.

❑ Check that commas enhance clarity, not clutter the sentence. If you're using a comma "just in case," double-check the rule to see if it's actually needed.

Fix Dangling Modifiers (Grammar)

A modifier is a word or phrase that describes (modifies) another word or phrase. A dangling modifier occurs when the thing being modified doesn't appear in the sentence or appears but not directly after the modifier.

Laughing loudly, the movie was over.

The modifier is "laughing loudly," but we never learn who that's describing. Who was laughing loudly?

While walking to work, a police car whizzed by.

The modifier is "walking to work," but we have no idea who was doing that walking.

After writing, the dogs needed to get outside for a walk.

This sounds like the dogs were writing. Pretty smart dogs.

Flashing lightning and thunder, the little bunny struggled through the storm.

Wow. That's one cool bunny! It can flash lightning and boom thunder. In this one, the word being modified (storm) does appear in the sentence, but it needs to come after the modifier.

Dangling modifiers often happen when the sentence starts with an –ing word or a while/after/before/by/during phrase. You can fix dangling modifiers in one of two ways:

- Name the subject after the modifier
- Put the subject into the modifier

So if we take this dangling modifier, "While reading the newspaper, the cat jumped on the table," we can fix it with:

- While **I** read the newspaper, the cat jumped on the table (put subject in the modifier).
- While reading the newspaper, **I had** to get the cat off the table.

Self-editing in practice

Original:

> The wind picked up as Anya walked toward the old lighthouse. Dark clouds gathered overhead, and she quickened her pace. After climbing the rocky path for twenty minutes, the lighthouse door came into view. She fumbled with the heavy brass key her grandmother had given her.
>
> Anya pushed open the weathered door. The smell of salt and dust hit her immediately. Looking around the circular room, old photographs covered every surface. Her grandmother had been the lighthouse keeper here for thirty years, and the memories felt thick in the air.
>
> Thunder crashed outside. While examining a faded photograph of ships, she jumped as rain began pelting the windows. Anya climbed the narrow spiral staircase to reach the lamp room at the

top. Breathing heavily from the climb, the view from the windows was breathtaking despite the storm.

She found what she was looking for—her grandmother's journal—sitting on a small wooden desk. Opening to the first page, she trembled. Tears welled up in Anya's eyes as she read her grandmother's familiar handwriting. The entries detailed daily life at the lighthouse, including weather observations and notes on passing ships.

A particularly loud crack of thunder made her jump. Startled by the sound, the journal slipped from her hands and scattered loose pages across the floor. Anya knelt to gather them up. While collecting the papers, a hidden compartment in the desk caught her attention (generated by ChatGPT).

PAUSE HERE

Open your personalized workbook on your computer and review the practice exercise, asking

- Does the sentence begin with a modifying phrase (–ing word or a "while/after/before/by/during" phrase)?

- Is the very next noun the one actually performing that action?

- If not, which fix makes more sense—adding the real subject after the modifier or putting the subject directly into the modifier?

After answering, make the needed changes, then check my revised version.

Revised:

The wind picked up as Anya walked toward the old lighthouse. Dark clouds gathered overhead, and she quickened her pace. After **she climbed** the rocky path for twenty minutes, the lighthouse door came into view. She fumbled with the heavy brass key her grandmother had given her.

Anya pushed open the weathered door. The smell of salt and dust hit her immediately. Looking around the circular room, **she took in the** old photographs covering every surface. Her grandmother had been the lighthouse keeper here for thirty years, and the memories felt thick in the air.

Thunder crashed outside. While examining a faded photograph of ships, she jumped as rain began pelting the windows. Anya climbed the narrow spiral staircase to reach the lamp room at the top. Breathing heavily from the climb, **she paused**. The view from the windows was breathtaking despite the storm.

She found what she was looking for—her grandmother's journal— sitting on a small wooden desk. Opening to the first page, she trembled. Tears welled up in Anya's eyes as she read her grandmother's familiar handwriting. The entries detailed daily life at the lighthouse, including weather observations and notes on passing ships.

A particularly loud crack of thunder made her jump. Startled by the sound, **she dropped the journal**, loose pages **scattering across the floor**. Anya knelt to gather them up. While collecting the papers, **she spotted** a hidden compartment in the desk.

EDITING STEPS

❑ Look for sentences that start with either an –ing verb or a phrase that describes the time, reason, or method something was done (while, after, before, by, during).

❑ Make sure the next word after the modifying phrase is the subject being modified.

❑ If it isn't, fix it by either naming the subject after the modifier or putting the subject in the modifier.

If you haven't done so yet, scan the QR code or visit: https://beaconpointservices.org/generate-fiction-personalized-workbook.

FEEDBACK PASS

You open your critique partner's notes and immediately think, *They didn't get it*. Five minutes later, you realize . . . they either nailed it or completely missed the point.

When you're reading feedback on your manuscript, you don't have to agree with every comment, but you should at least consider each one.

- **Critique Partner:** Gives more in-depth feedback as a writer, and in exchange, you critique their work.
- **Beta Readers:** Give you feedback as a reader, not as a writer (they can be writers, but they're giving you feedback as readers).

Do you need critique partners and/or beta readers?

The feedback pass helps you get a reader's perspective; something you can never have as the author. What makes sense to you may not make sense to a reader, so it's in your best interest to get feedback from others to get your manuscript in the best shape possible before enlisting an editor. Of course, you don't have to use either. However, the stronger your manuscript is before you send it to an editor, the less time (and money) you'll spend, and the better the final product will be.

How to find good feedback partners

This question is really out of the scope of this book, but you should check out *Finding the Write Fit* by Ross Lampert. It'll guide you in finding good critique partners and beta readers.

After that, you can read Lampert's entire Craft & Critique book series, which starts with *Giving and Receiving Effective Critique.* (Find the link to these and other resources in appendix B.)

Applying feedback

Wait until you have received feedback from all your readers before implementing any of it. Yes, people will finish at different times, but resist the temptation to revise until you have gathered all the feedback.

ORGANIZE

First, compile all the feedback into one place: a Word document, an Excel spreadsheet, a Notes app, etc.

Once compiled, group similar comments together. Create categories like feedback on specific chapters, particular concepts, overall impressions, writing style, etc.

Grouping makes it easier to spot common themes. If multiple readers flag the same chapter or concept, that's a clear sign something isn't working and deserves closer attention.

EVALUATE AND FILTER

With everything grouped by category (story, scene, writing style, chapter 5, etc.), decide which comments truly don't fit your vision and set them aside. If it's a common theme, pause and ask whether it's your ego talking. You may love a specific section, but if several readers struggle with it, pay attention.

Ultimately, you get to decide what to implement and what to ignore. My only advice is to give each piece of feedback real consideration without letting your ego interfere. Ask whether the suggestion would genuinely strengthen the manuscript. And if you need to, let the feedback sit for a while before you make a decision.

You aren't going to please everyone, so you don't need to take every opinion to heart. Remove feedback that doesn't resonate with or serve your vision, and keep the rest.

PRIORITIZE

Once you have filtered the list, tackle the big-picture feedback first and save the more minor details for later. For instance, if readers feel confused by a concept in chapter 3, fix that before worrying about smoothing out transition sentences.

It's helpful not only to list what you'll tackle first, but also to arrange those items in manuscript order. For example, address big-picture feedback for chapter 1 before tackling big-picture feedback for chapter 6.

DIVE IN

Now work through your list and make the changes. Trust your judgment, stay open to improvement, and remember, this feedback is helping you create the strongest version of your book. Once you have implemented the feedback that serves your vision, you'll have a manuscript that's reader-tested and ready for the next stage: professional editing.

OTHER FEEDBACK

Certain topics benefit from feedback from a sensitivity reader—someone with lived experience in a particular area who reviews your manuscript for potentially harmful, inaccurate, or stereotypical representations. Their goal is to help you avoid unintentional harm.

If your book deals with mental health conditions, trauma and abuse, disability and chronic illness, cultural or religious topics outside your experience, LGBTQ+ experiences, and different races and ethnicities, it's a good idea to get a sensitivity check.

Keep in mind that one sensitivity reader doesn't represent an entire community. If you're writing about a complex topic, consider hiring multiple sensitivity readers when your budget allows. Each person's lived experience matters, but perspectives within any group vary widely.

EDITING STEPS

- ❑ Compile all feedback in one place.
- ❑ Group similar comments together by category:
  - Chapters
  - Concepts
  - Overall impressions
  - Writing style
  - Other themes
- ❑ Identify common themes.
- ❑ Review feedback category by category and remove any feedback that doesn't resonate or serve your vision. (Pause and reflect on feedback and consider first whether it's valid.)
- ❑ Create an editing checklist that addresses big-picture feedback first (story, character, scenes), then handles smaller details (writing and technical details).
  - Optional: Arrange feedback in manuscript order.
- ❑ Work through prioritized feedback one at a time.

CONCLUSION

Whew! You made it.

If you feel overwhelmed with the self-editing process, I get it. I'm overwhelmed by the idea of writing an entire novel. It took so much effort just to write the examples in this book (the ones I did write) and then edit them to illustrate each technique. Creating an entire plot and characters is like wizardry to me, which is why I stick to editing!

So really, you already did something super hard. You wrote a whole novel. So now you've got this!

Writing a book is brave. Self-editing one is braver. I've heard from many authors that editing took them longer than actually writing their manuscript. And they're not alone. Many well-known authors have said some version of "good writing is rewriting!" No one's unedited draft comes out brilliant. None of them.

If you've made it this far, you've proven you're committed not just to finishing a manuscript but to becoming a stronger, more thoughtful writer. So just remember to take it slowly, and don't try to edit for everything. Two or three topics per pass are enough. Then incorporate feedback from your beta readers and get your manuscript off to an editor.

I hope the techniques and tools I talked about, plus those listed in appendices A and B, stay with you long after you close this book. That way, when you sit down to self-edit your next book, you'll already have a process—and a partner in these pages—to guide you.

Keep going. Your stories matter, and the world needs the light only you can offer. So use my free gift to you (see the next page) to publish your book so the world can hear from you.

Keep shining your beacon brightly,

Katie Chambers

GIFT FOR YOU
The Professional Editing Roadmap

You did it! You self-edited your whole manuscript. Take a second and enjoy that. If that superhuman pose, piece of pie, or dancing that you did before you self-edited worked, do it again. Or take your celebration to the next level: throw on the most amazing outfit in your closet, cue up your favorite song, and dance in every room in your house, or perform a victory lap around your entire neighborhood, screaming "I'm amazing."

After the celebration, it's time for the next step: professional editing. That might sound easy: find an editor, hand off your draft, and relax.

But

- Do you know how to find the right editor for your book?
- Do you know what red and green flags to look for and what questions to ask before hiring them?
- Once the edits come back, are you ready for markup you didn't expect?
- Do you know how to revise and rewrite based on external feedback?
- Do you know how much time and money to budget for and how to work on a limited budget?

If you answered yes to all of those, great! But if you'd like some help, I've got you.

I'm offering a free gift to all authors who picked up this book—The Professional Editing Roadmap: 6 Steps to Hiring the Right Editor, Navigating the Editing Process, and Getting the Most From Your Investment.

This free six-step email course gives you everything you need to go into the editing process informed and confident:

- **Step 1: What to Expect When Working with an Editor.** This debunks 10 common false assumptions about editing and replaces them with realistic expectations, so you know exactly what the author-editor relationship will look like from the start.

- **Step 2: Inside the Editor's Studio.** This breaks down the four levels of editing so you know exactly what your book needs (and what you'll be hiring and paying for).

- **Step 3: How Much Will This Be Again?** This is where I'll break down why editing costs what it does, a workable budget, and some smart strategies when you're in a rush or money is tight.

- **Step 4: From Start to Finish.** This lays out the entire editing process ahead of time so you can have a bird's-eye view of what happens from first search to final returned edits.

- **Step 5: Responding, Revising, and Rewriting.** This digs into dealing with Tracked Changes, making informed choices based on editor's suggestions, and even pushing back when you disagree (it will happen, and it's okay when it does!).

- **Step 6: The Right Editor for Me.** This brings everything together to help you understand exactly who you're looking for to make *your* book the best it can be (and what it looks like when you find them!).

This email course will teach you everything you need to know to find, hire, and work with not just any editor, but the perfect one for your book. Not every editor will walk you through all of that. This course will.

Sign up free at https://beaconpointservices.org/get-free-resource/ or scan the QR code below.

Reader Bonus: 50% off the Author Management Tracker

(NORMALLY $29 — YOUR PRICE: $14.50)

The Author Management Tracker gives you a single, organized system to manage your journey.

Built in Excel, it replaces scattered notes and multiple homemade spreadsheets with one clear place to track your progress, deadlines, and budget as you move through editing, publishing, and launch—so you're not constantly wondering what's next or what you might be forgetting.

Get access to your free Professional Editing Roadmap and your reader-only discount by scanning the QR code or visiting https://beaconpointservices.org/get-free-resource/.

Now You Get the Red Pen

Share your feedback by reviewing on Amazon and/or Goodreads.

Any review—good, neutral, or "Katie, what were you thinking?"—helps other readers decide if this book is right for them.

Just a few honest sentences can help a future reader decide whether to invest their time and money.

If I survived 8th graders, I can survive honest feedback. So tell it straight.

I'll just be over here, refreshing my dashboard and appreciating you more than you know.

AMAZON

GOODREADS

ABOUT THE AUTHOR

Katie Chambers is a developmental editor and copyeditor and the owner of Beacon Point LLC, where she helps fiction authors strengthen story, structure, and voice. She's known for spotting plot holes, improving interiority, and elevating writing craft so every thread weaves together into a cohesive, compelling narrative.

Before editing, Katie taught middle and high school English, where she developed a deep love for analyzing craft. That teacher brain still shows up in her work: her edits model technique directly in the manuscript and explain the "why" behind the changes so authors grow more confident with every revision.

When she's not editing, you'll find her reading, eating out, snuggling with her cats, cooking, or hanging out with her supportive husband and their three kids.

Learn more and explore free resources at beaconpointservices.org.

APPENDIX A

Beacon Point Resources

If you're unsure what topics to edit for or how to apply them to your manuscript, check out these two options for more guided self-editing.

Manuscript Checkup service

I charge a flat $500 for this bridge service. This service is for authors who want professional feedback to help guide their self-editing and save time and money before getting full editing or submitting to an agent.

I will

- professionally edit your first 10k words
- provide a detailed letter on what's working and where you need to focus your editing attention
- provide a one-on-one coaching call, teaching you how to edit for specific craft techniques your manuscript needs, walking you through my thinking process and how I go about making edits in your manuscript (since I will have only seen the first 10k words, I can't assess the top two in each pass. I can only go off the 10k words to determine the greatest needs. If granted permission, I can run your manuscript through my custom diagnostic AI tool explained below, then use the rubric to help guide the coaching call, but I can also do this service without using my tool)

- provide feedback for one self-revised chapter after the coaching call, so you know you're applying the techniques well

Self-Editing Diagnostic tool

This tool is being designed (will be coming out in 2026) to help authors identify their top revision priorities by analyzing patterns across an entire manuscript and mapping them to the editing topics covered in this book.

The goal is not to replace editorial judgment or hands-on revision, but to help you focus your time and energy where it will make the biggest difference and to offer individualized guidance on how to apply self-editing techniques more effectively in relation to your manuscript.

HOW IT'S INTENDED TO WORK

When available, the diagnostic tool will:

Highlight editing priorities. Using a rubric aligned with this guide—along with clearly defined analysis questions, clear indicators of strengths, and common weak flags (I wrote all of them)—the tool will identify which editing topics are most likely to need attention in your manuscript.

Provide a clear scorecard. Rather than vague feedback, the tool will offer a structured overview showing which areas appear strong and which would benefit from focused revision in each pass.

Illustrate issues with examples. Where helpful, the tool will surface short excerpts from your manuscript to illustrate specific craft issues for each lower-scoring topic in each pass. These examples are meant to support learning, not to overwrite your voice or dictate revisions.

A NOTE ABOUT AI AND ANALYSIS

Although this tool uses AI as the customer-facing interface to present results clearly and in plain language, AI is not acting as the editor. The analysis itself is based on structured criteria drawn from this guide, with my editorial oversight and coding. The underlying system evaluates patterns and indicators in your manuscript, while AI is used to explain the results and reasoning in a clear, readable way.

Think of AI here as the messenger, not the decision-maker.

PRIVACY PROTECTION

Your manuscript remains your intellectual property, and protecting it is central to how this tool is being designed.

- Your full manuscript is not reviewed by a conversational, chat-based AI. It *will not* see your manuscript. While you upload your file through an AI-based interface, the manuscript itself is processed by a separate off-site diagnostic system designed specifically for this analysis.
- Only short excerpts may be reviewed by AI, and only when necessary to explain a specific craft issue. These excerpts are kept to a minimum.
- Your writing is not used to train AI models. Your content is not added to any dataset or reused in any way.
- Files are stored only as long as needed to generate your report or resolve technical issues.

Visit https://beaconpointservices.org/author-products/#diagnostic to sign up to be notified when the tool is ready or scan the QR code.

I've finished self-editing, now what?

Congratulations! You've strengthened your manuscript and grown as a writer.

If you're ready to hire an editor, I'd love for you to consider my team and me. You need to feel good about the editor you go with, and we're not the right editor for everyone. So, do reach out to a few editors to determine the best fit for you.

We offer a sample edit and/or discovery call to help determine if we're the right fit. Just go to scan the QR code or visit https://beaconpointservices.org/editing-fiction-authors and fill out a request form.

Genres Beacon Point edits

- Young adult fantasy, dystopian, supernatural, mystery, and thriller
- Adult dystopian, mystery, thriller (clean content)
- Children's picture books and chapter books
- Middle-grade novels
- Members of my team can edit
- Historical fiction (young adult and adult)
- Closed-door romance
- Poetry
- Science fiction (young adult and adult)

I can refer you to an editor if you have a horror, literary fiction, dark romance, erotica, or graphic novel. Just email me.

Rates & Services

*These are my rates at the time of publishing this book. If my rates have increased, just mention you read this book, and I'll honor these rates.

Developmental Editing, $0.03–$0.05 per word: Deals with plot, characters, scenes, and some narrative techniques. Includes an editorial letter.

Copyediting, $0.02–$0.035 per word: Deals with word- and sentence-level issues, both narrative technique and general word choice and fixing errors.

Combined Package, $0.035–$0.065 per word: Combines both types of editing in one round for a discounted rate to meet authors' budgetary constraints

Manuscript Checkup, $500: A bridge service for authors who want professional feedback to help guide their self-editing and save time and money before getting full editing or submitting to an agent.

APPENDIX B

Additional Resources for You

Being an author, especially a self-published one, involves a lot. So, to help you through the process, I have curated resources for you. You can also check out the resource center on my website, which mentions all the ones below plus my free blogs, webinars, and courses; recommended service providers; and more: https://beaconpointservices.org/writing-resources/.

If you're going the traditional route, several resources still apply to you, though some are specific to self-publishing.

I've grouped the resources by topic:

- Assisted self-publishing companies
- Networking and learning
- Writing craft
- Grammar, punctuation, and spelling help
- Feedback pass help
- Marketing help
- Audiobook narration
- More self-editing help

ASSISTED SELF-PUBLISHING COMPANIES

You need to be careful to avoid assisted self-publishing scams. Unfortunately, a lot of bad actors are masquerading as hybrid publishers, but they take your money and don't do much for you. These are all companies I've personally vetted; of course, you can find plenty of other good ones.

JWC Publishing: https://www.jacobswc.com

Precocity Press: https://www.precocitypress.com

Bedside Reading: https://www.bedsidereading.com/publishing.html

SWATT Books: https://swatt-books.co.uk

Archangel Ink: http://bit.ly/2FrrXuB (my affiliate link)

Stellar Houston Communications: https://stellarwriter.com/publishing

Jennifer Wilkov's Done-For-You Publishing: https://yourbookisyourhook.com/services/collaborative-services/book-done-for-you

Ghostwriters Network Publishing: https://ghostwritersnetwork.com/get-published

Credible Ink: https://www.credible.ink/

NETWORKING AND LEARNING

Each of these communities includes networking and learning opportunities.

Alliance of Independent Authors ($119 a year): They "campaign for author rights and offer tailored education, trusted resources, and a global community so you can publish and sell with confidence."

https://www.allianceindependentauthors.org/members/join?affid=21111 (my affiliate link)

Twin Flame Studios (free): They host live expert panels and Q&A sessions covering every topic imaginable in the industry. You can register for these free panels on their website. Just go to "Live Events." They also have a directory of curated industry professionals (go to "Author Resources").

https://twinflamesstudios.com/audiobook-services/?nowprocket=1partnerid=r1675 (my partner link)

Quill & Cup ($47 a month with a free 7-day trial): A woman-centered writing community to help you improve your craft, strengthen your mindset, and make progress on your writing. Members receive expert coaching and twice-weekly lessons, daily accountability, a library of webinars and workshops (over 100 hours of learning), and more.

https://www.quillandcup.com/offers/ZtsLiHPG/checkout
(my affiliate link)

The Writer's Workout (free): A community of writers from different backgrounds and skill levels. Members receive a minicourse on foundational writing, a yearly free conference, entrance to competitions and games, and more.

https://www.writersworkout.net

WRITING CRAFT

Crafting Beautiful Prose (£45): Voice, originality, and style … are skills that can be developed. You don't have to be born with it! This 50-minute webinar will give you practical tips for creating lyricism in your writing.

https://www.liminalpages.com/webinars/crafting-beautiful
-prose?mc_cid=3e52742e66&mc_eid=34eadae4c3

Writers Helping Writers: Becca Puglisi and Angela Ackerman run this free hub of craft resources for fiction writers, including an extensive library of blog content covering plot, characters, world-building, revision, show-don't-tell, and more (the link below takes you to the blog navigation). It's also home to free downloadable tools and worksheets.

https://writershelpingwriters.net/plot-structure/

One Stop for Writers ($11 a month or $105 a year): Writers helping writers, Becca Puglisi and Angela Ackerman, created this companion software platform, giving fiction writers access to 23 thesauruses, a character builder, story maps, worldbuilding surveys, an idea generator, and a writing coach roadmap—all in one place.

https://onestopforwriters.com/

Helping Writers Become Authors: Award-winning author K.M. Weiland runs one of the most comprehensive free craft blogs available, with over a decade of in-depth posts covering story structure, character arcs, outlining, scene structure, theme, and more. Weiland also offers several acclaimed craft books, a free Story Structure Database, and a podcast.

https://www.helpingwritersbecomeauthors.com/

GRAMMAR, PUNCTUATION, AND SPELLING HELP

Given the wide range of this topic, I didn't cover these topics in depth. If you're interested in expanding your learning, check out these resources.

***Tricky Quickies* Series by Debbie Emmitt (£5.99–7.99):** These books "clearly and concisely explain similar, everyday English words and phrases, with handy examples of use."

> https://www.debbie-emmitt.com/books-and-resources/tricky-quickies/

Grammar Girl (free): She "provides short, friendly tips to improve your writing and feed your love of the English language."

> https://www.quickanddirtytips.com/grammar-girl

Grammar Conundrums Course by Catherine Turner ($27): "Grammar Conundrums includes tons of example sentences so you can see these tricky words in action AND 750 quiz questions to help you lock in that knowledge forever."

> https://turnerproofreading.com/grammar-conundrums

Punctuation 101 eBook and Workbook by Catherine Turner ($17): "An ebook and workbook combo that'll help you refresh your memory of punctuation rules, learn the punctuation mistakes you need to avoid making, and polish your punctuation skills so you can wow your readers."

> https://turnerproofreading.com/punctuation-101

FEEDBACK PASS HELP

Learn how to receive and give effective critique from the Critique Doctor, Ross Lampert.

Finding the Write Fit: The Critique Doctor's guide to finding the critique partnership that works for you (Craft & Critique Book 0)

https://books2read.com/u/mYO8wY

Giving and Receiving Effective Critique: The Critique Doctor's guide to helping other writers write better (and still be your friends) (Craft & Critique Book 1)

https://books2read.com/u/49Grld

Mechanics, Narrative, and Description: The Critique Doctor's guide to helping other writers (and yourself) create clear, compelling prose (Craft & Critique Book 2)

https://books2read.com/u/4NOogJ

MARKETING

This is often the hardest yet most important step for authors to learn. Check out these resources to help you.

Book Marketing Webinar by Teddy Smith and Aryn Van Dyke (free): It covers how to master your book launch, leverage AI to supercharge your Amazon ads, engage your audience and build buzz, and learn how other authors transformed their sales using these methods.

https://www.youtube.com/watch?v=5HsijrfNRgg

Book Sirens ($10 one-time fee plus $2 per reader OR $100 a year for multiple books): Find ARC readers from their 51,000+ book reviewers and influencers and grow your mailing list.

https://booksirens.com/?affiliate=DTX0NV8 (my affiliate link)

Booksprout (plans ranging from $9 to $29 a month): Find ARC readers from their 90,000 active reviewers.

https://booksprout.co/?ref=katie-chambers38
(my affiliate link, which gets you a free month)

Book PR Checklist by Bianca Sanders (free): This is a cheat sheet to book PR to get you started on your marketing journey.

https://www.myrtileditorial.com/bookprchecklist

Improve Your Author Website by **Debbie Emmitt (£9.95):** This guide will help you improve your author website to attract readers and agents, move up in search results, and look polished and professional.

https://www.debbie-emmitt.com/improve-your-author-website

Author Marketing & Launch Notion Planner by Shelly Zevlever (CAD $6.99): This Notion page is set up to accompany you across the process of setting up your social media accounts, getting ready for launch, and all the details in between that help you market your book.

https://shellyzev.com/author-marketing-and-launch

Book Award Pro (plans ranging from free to $69 a month): They operate the world's largest database of legitimate reviews and awards and match you up with the awards that are right for your book.

https://bookawardpro.com

David Gaughran's newsletter. Sign up for his valuable marketing newsletter and get a free marketing book and course.

https://davidgaughran.com/following-free-newsletter/

AUDIOBOOK NARRATION

If your book lends itself well to audiobook format, you're leaving money on the table but not looking into it.

Narrate Your Own Book minicourse by professional actor David H. Lawrence XVII (free): This free minicourse will help you understand how to become the voice of your own audiobook.

https://narrateyourownbook.com

Narrate Your Own Book Course by professional actor David H. Lawrence XVII ($1,995 or three monthly payments of $697): The course walks you through preparing your manuscript for audiobook format, creating your home studio equipment (he provides the equipment), learning voice acting skills, handling the production workflow, and releasing and marketing your new audiobook.

https://go.narrateyourownbook.com/referral/nyob/
euVYnrsalHmxICog (my affiliate link)

Connect with an Audience of Millions Using the Power of Your Audiobook by Tina Dietz of Twin Flame Studios (free): Learn tips to make the audiobook process easier and what options can save you time and money. Plus, learn how to turn your audiobook into content that drives more book and audio sales.

> https://twinflamesstudios.com/connect/?partnerid=r1675
> (my affiliate link)

Audiobook production services by Twin Flames Studio: They will do the editing, mastering, proofing, distributing, and marketing for your audiobook. They offer two options: author as narrator (they provide remote support and direction on performance and tech) or professional as narrator (they have a network of 7,000+).

> https://twinflamesstudios.com/audiobook-services/?nowprocket=
> 1partnerid=r1675 (my affiliate link)

SELF-EDITING

While this is what my book covered, you can never have too much knowledge or tools to help you with this task. Two of my colleagues have courses that teach authors how to self-edit.

Reader Ready Revisions course by Olivia Bedford ($696): This course combined the flexibility of a self-paced course with the professional feedback and support of a live one.

> https://www.oliviahelpswriters.com/reader-ready-revisions

From First Draft to Final Product: Self-Editing Tools for Every Stage of Your Manuscript ($190): This course is taught through the EFA by

Jeanette Smith. It covers self-editing mindset, the knowledge you need to edit, and some writing and editing tools.

https://courses.the-efa.org/courses/126910

Fictionary StoryTeller (Plans start at $14 a month): This is a scene-by-scene structural editing software that guides fiction writers through outlining, writing, and revising using 38 story elements covering plot, character, and setting.

https://fictionary.co/products/storyteller/

APPENDIX C

Master Self-Editing Checklist

If you want a printable master list, you can go to https://beaconpointservices.org/generate-fiction-personalized-workbook and download a PDF master checklist.

Story Pass

Pick the best point of view

❑ Identify the current POV: omniscient, first, or third.

❑ Reread three important scenes (including your climax and a turning point) and assess them for all the POV considerations:

- Does the current POV create the emotional impact you intended? If not, consider a POV with deeper intimacy.
- Do the scenes feel constricted by a specific character voice? If so, consider using third person instead of first.
- Is your current POV forcing you to use contrived situations (overheard conversations, convenient observations, flashbacks) to convey information? If so, consider using a different POV entirely or a different POV character. You can also delete those situations entirely and let them happen off page.

❑ Check for red flags that may signal POV mismatch (either different POV or different POV characters).
- Frequent head hopping or unclear viewpoint
- Explanations the POV character wouldn't naturally think
- Overexplaining or awkward justification for giving the reader information
- Disorientation caused by switching too often between characters

❑ Run the rewrite test. Choose one pivotal scene and rewrite it in a different POV (first, third, or omniscient).
- Which version feels more alive?
- Which version reveals tension, emotion, and characterization more effectively?
- Which version aligns better with the themes or tone you're aiming for?

❑ If you have multiple POV characters, list every character who has a POV scene. Mark how often they appear as a narrator. If someone has fewer than three scenes as a POV character or if long stretches pass between their appearances, strongly reconsider whether they're truly necessary as a POV character.

❑ Make the POV decision and any necessary revisions to comply with it:
- Which POV will you use (current POV or a different one)?
- What characters will be POV characters?

Follow a plot structure

❑ Choose a framework (three-act structure, Hero's Journey, Story Circle, etc.) to guide your analysis.

❑ Outline your story's plot using your chosen framework, labeling each major plot point with its intended part of the structure (this helps you see whether your story aligns with the framework).

❑ Analyze your story for the structure:

- • Do any major plot points occur too early or too late in the story?
- • Are any essential plot points missing or not fully fleshed out?
- • Do any plot points last too long?
- ❏ Delete or revise plot points that don't match the structure.
- ❏ Add in any missing plot points.
- ❏ Shorten plot points that are too long and lengthen any that are too short (a lot of the "how" to do this is covered in the writing pass, as this often comes down to the word and sentence level).

Establish and escalate your story's central conflict

- ❏ Identify your central conflict in one sentence: "The protagonist wants X, but Y stands in the way, and if they fail, Z happens." If you can't articulate this clearly, neither can your reader, and you need to go back and clarify your central conflict.
- ❏ Is your central conflict clear within the first few chapters? If not, cut out some of the fluff before the conflict or move the conflict earlier.
- ❏ Does your central conflict resolve at or very near the climax, or does it fizzle out earlier?
- ❏ List your major plot complications and check them for effectiveness:
  - • Are your rising complications all tied to the central conflict, or do they feel unrelated?
  - • Are the stakes higher in act 3 than they were in act 1?
  - • Does the protagonist face a harder choice at the climax than at the inciting incident?
  - • Does the final confrontation (external and/or internal) feel like the ultimate test?
  - • Do the stakes feel personal or too generic?
- ❏ If you answered no to any of the above, revise to strengthen the escalation.

Create cause-and-effect chains

- ❑ Ask cause-and-effect questions for each scene: What caused this event, and what effect does this event have on the story or character?
- ❑ If a scene doesn't follow a causal thread, revise or delete.
  - If the scene can advance the plot, reveal character, or show relationships, consider keeping it and strengthening the causal link or deleting it and showing the advancement and characterization in a different scene.
  - If it doesn't reveal character or show relationships, delete it.

Ensure plot continuity

- ❑ Ask questions to check for contradictions, unexplained events, illogical events, impossible events, and/or unresolved events within a scene and throughout the story thread:
  - Does the story present two facts that can't both be true?
  - Do any events occur without sufficient setup or explanation?
  - Do any objects, places, or plot devices appear without any hint of origin or cause?
  - Would a reader reasonably expect an explanation for an event that wasn't delivered?
  - Do any major outcomes feel unearned or implausible based on what the story has established?
  - Are there moments when the plot conveniently solves itself without enough groundwork?
  - Do any plot points feel too easy, lucky, or forced?
  - Do any events break the internal logic or rules of the story world?
  - Did any subplots remain unresolved?
  - At the end of the story, do any lingering questions remain that a reader would expect to have been addressed?
- ❑ Revise any issues spotted.

❑ Use beta readers to find plot holes that you were too close to the manuscript to see.

Organize the timeline effectively

❑ Track your timeline. (You can do this however you want.)
❑ Highlight any discrepancies in the timeline. (I do this by highlighting problematic days or events in the tracked chart.)
❑ Make changes to ensure the timeline matches up.

Make characters believable

❑ Ensure each major character has a believable, unique personality:
  • Does the character have both strengths and weaknesses?
  • Can you explain how their past shaped their personality?
  • Can you identify defining traits that separate them from other characters?
❑ Anytime a character "acts out of character," either ensure a clear catalyst exists or change that moment for them to act true to character, even if that changes the plot point.
❑ For each major decision, reaction, or moment of judgment, ensure logical thinking for their current emotional state:
  • Does their conclusion make sense based on the information they have?
  • Is their emotional response tied to their backstory, wounds, or personality?
  • Do they eventually reassess once their emotional spike settles?
❑ For each scene, add in selective reactions if the character isn't grounded:
  • Does the character respond to what's happening around them?
  • Do they occasionally notice or interpret something based on their mood, fear, stress, or internal conflict?
  • Are they a participant in the scene rather than a talking head?

Ensure characters are dynamic

❑ Check each scene to ensure the main character has a clear, small goal that leads to the overall goal. If they don't, revise to give the protagonist a goal in that scene and add stakes if they don't meet it (the motivation they need).

❑ Check that the character creates meaningful change in each scene through their choices, driven by their desire to achieve their goal. If they don't, increase the pressure on them and create a clear choice.

❑ Verify that your character makes a deliberate choice at the inciting incident or turning points and then continues to choose that path (or double down on it) as conflicts test them.

❑ Ensure your character makes both good and bad choices, maybe even making them culpable for the fallout.

❑ If your character is lacking overall change, diagnose the gap by asking:
  - What theme are you exploring in your novel?
  - How is the character initially misaligned with that theme?
  - What events will force them to shift toward (or away from) this theme by the end?
  - How does the external plot pressure or mirror this internal shift?

❑ Map your character's arc: Identify who they are at the beginning and who they are at the end. Identify two or three key moments when they should show signs of this transformation and add those in.

Create good secondary characters

❑ Write down each side character's function in a given scene. If they lack purpose, cut them out or revise to give them one.

❑ Ensure each side character has one to three defining characteristic(s) that remain consistent throughout and that they have a life of their own.

❑ Read through scenes where side characters are prominent and ask, Is this scene ultimately about the MC's journey, even if the side character is more active? If yes, keep it. If no, revise or cut.

❑ Ensure the MC has a strong internal experience in these scenes. Are we in their head, feeling their reaction, watching them change? Or are they just a camera observing the side character?

❑ Do the side characters have their own subplot that readers get invested in that doesn't help or hinder the MC in any way? If yes, drop it entirely or shorten it and weave it into specific moments.

Scene Pass

Craft strong entry and exit points

❑ Identify the purpose of the scene—introduce conflict or goal, reveal something about the point of view (POV) character, etc.—and ensure the entry point aligns with that purpose.

❑ Ensure you're starting *in medias res*—in the middle of the action or situation that matters.

- Action can be internal (conflict, decision, fear) or external (dialogue, confrontation, event).
- Don't confuse "start with action" with a full-on chaotic, action-packed scene.
- Locate where the true action and tension begin and cut any fluff or throat-clearing that doesn't add essential plot or characterization.
- Orient us with a few clear, concrete details if you have shifted time and location. Include just enough to set tone and context, but not so much that it delays the action.

❑ Read the last few lines of the scene and ask, Does this leave something unresolved? If not, revise to end with

- a new conflict or obstacle
- a complication to the victory just achieved
- a decision or choice that carries consequences

- a discovery that changes the character's understanding
- a line of dialogue or image that hints at what's coming next

❏ Cut out any routine scene endings (drove home, went to bed, left the restaurant).

Structure with action and reaction

❏ If your story moves too fast, add short reflective beats after big moments (you may just need a few sentences of reaction). If your story drags, tighten or combine slower reactions so the action resumes before a reader's patience wears thin.
  - Optional idea: Color code your manuscript: one color for action sequences and another for reaction sequences. Now, zoom out and look at the color balance in your manuscript. If you have too much action or reflection in a row, weave in the missing balance.

❏ When your scene includes a reaction, make sure to include the reaction, the dilemma that follows, and the decision that moves them forward.

❏ Within your reaction sequences, ensure your character's emotions evolve. They shouldn't feel the same after every scene. If they do, the reaction sequence is just filler and should either be cut or replaced with a different reaction.

Build conflict and stakes

❏ Chart the goal, conflict, and stake for every scene or just those that feel flat.

❏ For those that don't have a clear conflict and/or stakes, revise the scene using a "yes, but" or "when, then, until" framework.

Generate microtension

☐ If a scene is structurally sound with a goal, conflict, stakes, and a scene ending that leaves the reader wanting more, but the scene itself feels flat, add in microtension, using a few different tactics:

- Something feels off: body language that doesn't match dialogue, a pause too long, an unspoken thought that shifts the tone
- References to something in the past (this morning, years ago, whatever) that get the reader curious and wondering
- Characters acting and speaking in ways that contradict their goals and desires
- Characters misinterpreting their own emotions
- Characters with conflicting emotions: pride under fear, affection under anger
- A character's emotional state influencing how they perceive and describe their surroundings
- Conversations containing interruptions, clipped responses, contradictory ideas, or silence
- Setting described in a way that builds tension
- Setting and scene that contradict the character's mood
- One character being uncertain or suspicious of the other

Writing Pass

Deepen interiority and close the narrative distance

☐ Use Word's Find feature to find filter words and remove them unless they aren't creating a distance or you're intentionally creating a wider distance.

☐ Identify scenes/moments when you want to close the distance and change the narration to reflect the character's voice: their reactions, vocabulary, attitudes, and what they would notice and care about.

❏ Identify scenes/moments that need deeper interiority and insert the character's thoughts and feelings.

❏ Use either free indirect speech, indirect thoughts, or direct thoughts as needed, knowing that free indirect speech closes the narrative distance the most.

❏ Make sure you don't overdo it and give us too much of the character's internal world.

❏ Make sure the thoughts are realistic and not just dumping information.

❏ Change some action beats showing character's emotions to thoughts instead.

Ensure point of view consistency

❏ Identify the POV character for each scene.

❏ Look for thoughts, emotions, and sensations attributed to any character that the POV character wouldn't realistically know.

❏ Decide what to do with that information:
  • If the information that comes through head hopping doesn't advance the plot, deepen the POV character, or enhance understanding of the scene, you can delete it.
  • If the head hopping is important, show it through the POV character's observations, interpretations, or reactions.

Master show and tell

❏ Search for filter words using Word's Find feature and rewrite to get rid of them. (You can also use a macro that will highlight all of them for you. AI is pretty good at creating macros.)

❏ Fix passages that tell emotions; instead, show them either through physical action beats or thoughts.

❏ Cut anything that explains a character's motivation, and show it instead.

❏ Use sensory details to show the character's perspective and scene mood.

❏ Fix longer chunks of told information by
  • deleting what isn't necessary to know in that moment
  • using natural dialogue, not "As you know, Bob" dialogue
  • putting the information in the character's voice and in a way that's natural for them to be thinking at that moment

❏ Integrate characters' backstories into the action throughout or delete if unnecessary.

Craft effective exposition

❏ Look for areas where you tell chunks of information without anything happening in the moment.

❏ Determine whether each of those areas is okay as is:
  • If it's brief, it's probably fine. You do need to tell some information.
  • If it's longer but stays in the character's voice, it's a shown info dump and is likely fine.

❏ Determine whether the reader must know that information in that moment. If they don't, delete that information from that scene and integrate it later when it's important to know.

❏ For any info dump that's necessary in the moment, fix it by
  • building a scene around it (just make sure you don't include any "As you know, Bob" dialogue)
  • building the information into an already existing scene
  • changing it to a shown info dump

Delete unnecessary explanations

❏ Search for explanation trigger words like "because," "so that," "in order to," "since," etc. Then delete the explanation if it's already clear from context.

❏ Read your dialogue and the narration that follows. If the narration repeats what the dialogue already reveals, delete it.

❑ Track repeated information (the same backstory, motivation, or detail). Keep the strongest instance (or instances, if a character would naturally reflect on it more than once) and delete the rest.

❑ Check any exposition after a showing moment and delete anything that repeats what the showing already revealed.

Strengthen dialogue

❑ Make sure all your dialogue either reveals character or advances the plot.

❑ Make sure your dialogue is natural by eliminating dialogue that contains

- characters telling each other things they already know (as you know, Bob)
- overly formal, always perfectly grammatical language
- content unnatural for the character to say in that moment (unrelated to their motivations and desires)
- dialogue exchanges that are always too perfect, where everyone always understands each other and lets each other finish their sentences (But be careful not to overdo this. We do want your dialogue to be more "perfect" than in real life to keep the forward momentum.)

❑ Check that a character's dialogue is unique to how the character would talk:

- Speech patterns
- Vocabulary
- Tone

Refine tags and beats

❑ Revise action beats and dialogue tags to ensure

- a good balance of beats and tags with a variety of placements
- minimal to no tagging when it's clear who's speaking

- limited to no adverbs
- action beats don't state unnecessary movement, unnecessary body parts, or what the dialogue or exposition already made clear
- variety of action beats rather than an overreliance on crutches

Strengthen word choice

❏ Use the Find feature in Word to search for common filter words and revise to eliminate them, unless their use is intentional to create a wider narrative distance.

❏ Stop when you encounter a body part and ask if you're unnecessarily naming it or if it's doing the action. If so, revise to fix that.

❏ Stop on sentences that use –ing verbs, "as," and "while" and make sure you haven't created any false simultaneity. Revise if so.

❏ Stop when a sentence (even short ones) feels like a mouthful and/or has several little words, and revise to avoid
- qualifiers
- prepositional phrases
- nominalizations
- adjectivizations
- expletive constructions
- unnecessary "which" or "that"

❏ Combine sentences that use "this" at the beginning of the second sentence.

❏ Check for sentence pairs you can combine using a colon and –ing word or by trimming portions.

Ensure good sentence fluency

❑ Pause when a section sounds flat, repetitive, or monotonous. (Don't just look at one paragraph. Read multiple paragraphs in the section to detect hidden rhythm issues.)

❑ Check your sentence beginnings: Do too many in a row follow the same beginning pattern even if the first word varies?

❑ Check the sentence lengths and types: Are most of the sentences the same length? Do they follow the same type?

❑ Revise with intentional variety if you answered yes to any of the above questions.

Eliminate excess "be" verbs

❑ Stop when a passage feels wordy, flat, or overly dependent on "be" verbs.

❑ Scan the section for an overuse of "be" verbs.

❑ Revise by reducing "be" verbs using any of the six strategies:

- Swap for a stronger verb
- Cut "be" verb and change –ing form of verb
- Show instead of tell
- Make another word in the sentence the verb
- Combine sentences
- Rearrange sentence order
- Get rid of unnecessary phrases.

Technical Pass

❑ Run general find-and-replace tasks

Correct easily confused words

❑ Use Word's Find feature to search for the first word in a pair you tend to confuse.
❑ For each result, check whether the word is used correctly in context.
❑ Search for the second word in the pair and review its usage.
❑ Repeat with each word pair you struggle with.

Ensure correct use of periods and commas with dialogue

❑ Zoom in so you can easily see the punctuation.
❑ Change any periods to commas if you have a dialogue tag before or after a line of dialogue.
❑ Change any commas to periods if you have an action beat before or after a line of dialogue.
❑ Change any commas to em dashes or periods if you have an action beat in the middle of a line of dialogue.

Ensure correct use of ellipses and em dashes in dialogue

❑ Find dialogue where you intended to show trailing off or an unintentional pause, and ensure you use ellipses.
❑ Find dialogue where you intended to show a speaker was interrupted either by another speaker or themselves, and ensure you use an em dash.
❑ Get rid of action beats that state the speaker trailed off or was interrupted, since the punctuation already shows that.
❑ Ensure any necessary action beat comes before, not after, the interrupted line of dialogue.

Fix common comma errors

❑ Watch out for run-ons. Check all coordinating conjunctions (FANBOYS) between two clauses. If each side could stand alone as its own sentence, insert a comma before the FANBOYS. If one side is a phrase (not a complete sentence), a comma usually isn't needed, though you can stylistically choose to have one.

❑ Watch out for comma splices. If two sentences are joined with just a comma, fix it by adding the missing FANBOYS or make it a period.

❑ Watch out for fused sentences. If two sentences aren't joined by anything, fix it by using one of the correct methods (comma and FANBOYS, semicolon, colon) or split it into two sentences with a period.

❑ Look at sentences with introductory words, clauses, or phrases. If a sentence starts with something before the main subject-verb clause, check if it needs a comma.

❑ Check that commas enhance clarity, not clutter the sentence. If you're using a comma "just in case," double-check the rule to see if it's actually needed.

Fix dangling modifiers

❑ Look for sentences that start with either an –ing verb or a phrase that describes the time, reason, or method something was done (while, after, before, by, during).

❑ Make sure the next word after the modifying phrase is the subject being modified.

❑ If it isn't, fix it by either naming the subject after the modifier or putting the subject in the modifier.

Feedback Pass

- ❏ Compile all feedback in one place.
- ❏ Group similar comments together by category:
    - chapters
    - concepts
    - overall impressions
    - writing style
    - other themes
- ❏ Identify common themes.
- ❏ Review feedback category by category and remove any feedback that doesn't resonate or serve your vision. (Pause and reflect on feedback and consider first whether it's valid.)
- ❏ Create an editing checklist that addresses big-picture feedback first (story, character, scenes), then handles smaller details (writing and technical details).
    - Optional: Arrange feedback in manuscript order.
- ❏ Work through prioritized feedback one at a time.

www.ingramcontent.com/pod-product-compliance
Lightning Source LLC
Chambersburg PA
CBHW071449140726
47997CB00005B/1654